SPILLOVER:

WAR IN

HEAVEN

A Study of Revelation 12

Wallace Henley

SPILLOVER: WAR IN HEAVEN

A Study of Revelation 12

Wallace Henley

SpiriTruth Publishing Company
Your source of discount digital publishing

Spillover: War In Heaven
Copyright © 2014
Wallace Henley

Published By:
SpirTruth Publishing Company
http://www.SpiriTruthPublishing.com
Email: spiritruthpublishing@gmail.com
Address: 7710-T Cherry Park Drive, Suite 224
Houston, Texas 77095 USA
Phone: (281) 830-8724

Printed in the United States of America

Unless otherwise noted all Scripture quotations are taken from THE NEW AMERICAN STANDARD BIBLE © The Lockman Foundation.

Ebook: 978-1-304-72174-7

Softcover: 978-1-304-72158-7

Hardcover: 978-1-304-87828-1

Table of Contents

THE 21ST CENTURY IS THE BEST OF TIMES TO

READ AND CONSUME THE *APOCALYPSE*

BECAUSE FOR THE FIRST TIME IN HISTORY

EVENTS AND CIRCUMSTANCES JOHN SAW IN HIS

REMARKABLE VISIONS ARE *GLOBALLY* POSSIBLE.

INTRODUCTION:
THE TWO KEYS THAT UNLOCK THE REVELATION

There's no time like the 21st century to do a deep dive into the Book of Revelation!

As I wrote in my previous book, *Globequake,* we are living in one of the most turbulent periods of history. We ride spiritual, moral, philosophical, political, commercial, educational (to name a few) "tectonic plates" that are redefining the whole world. Back in the age of literal tectonic shift, the plates crept across the planet's face by inches a century. But now they move at light-speed, and we are on top, trying to live our lives, raise and educate our families, work our jobs, build stable churches, elect trustworthy governments while the ground races beneath us and the landscape gets redefined constantly.

Multitudes believe we are living in the "end times." As a matter of fact, we are! The Bible shows it clearly and precisely, but it's not the "end" as many of us understand it. We will look at the riddle of the end in more detail in chapters to come.

Revelation has been hyped, hacked at, and huckstered since John's wiry, aged, shaky hand and trembling heart recorded his vision centuries ago. The 21st century is the best of times to read and consume the *Apocalypse* because for the

7

first time in history events and circumstances John saw in his remarkable visions are *globally* possible. There are at least nine of those prophecies Revelation showed would occur on a worldwide scale, and are for the first time not only probable, but are beginning to happen:

1. Global evangelization is possible and occurring because of rapid travel and communications. (Matthew 24:14)

2. Nations are aligning as foretold by the Prophet Ezekiel. (Ezekiel 38)

3. Global lawlessness is deepening through the impact of media and instantly transmitted social movements. (2 Thessalonians 2:1-12)

4. Revolution can now leap from nation to nation because of the ability to broadcast inciting images instantly. (Revelation 13:1; 17:15)

5. Apostasy in churches once faithful to the Gospel has grown to shocking proportions. (2 Thessalonians 2:1-3)

6. It is now possible to bring whole civilizations into delusion through global media. (2 Thessalonians 2:11; 2 Timothy 3:1-8)

7. For the first time in history it is possible for global markets to collapse in an "hour" because of the electronic economy. (Revelation 18)

8. Persecution of the genuine church is at unprecedented levels worldwide. (Matthew 24:9;Revelation 12)

9. War has shifted from conflicts between geopolitical entities to civilizational conflict. (Matthew 24:6-7)

However, even as we consider the "end," my hope is that in these pages you will see the Book of Revelation, not as a stirrer of blaring hysteria, but an inspirer of "blessed hope."

I've taught classes on the Book of Revelation for three decades or more. "I don't want to come to those Revelation studies because they scare me," I hear from a few every time I announce Revelation as the new study series. I agree: there's much to disturb and unsettle—*if you are on the wrong side.* But if you are in Christ and His Covenant, a citizen of the Kingdom of God, Revelation is thrilling, motivating, and charged with hope.

That's why right out of the chute, in Revelation 1:3, we read, "Blessed is he (and she) who reads the words of this prophecy..."

How can a person be "blessed" reading about demonic armies, ten-headed, seven-horned creatures, beasts rising from the sea, other monsters creeping on the ground, the blood of the martyrs, blasting war-trumpets, devilish frogs, pestilences, a collapsing global economy, rivers of blood, devastating winds, violent earthquakes, a deep abyss, and a lake of fire? The answer is in discovering what the Book of

Revelation is all about. That's what we will seek to do in this volume.

Vision, Values, Mission

My prayer is that through this book you will get an invigorating vision of the King and His Kingdom, and the way God's cosmic plan goes forward on two stages of time. You are an important part of this grand epic. I hope you will see how, where, and why you fit.

There are some strong values that guide me in this task, things I really care about as I write. Here are some of them:

- I value the Bible as God's revealed Word, inspired by the Holy Spirit without error, preserved by the Holy Spirit, illuminated for us by the Holy Spirit, and relevant for every facet of our lives and daily engagements, not just the "spiritual."
- I value the Triune Godhead—the Father as the Heart of the Trinity, the Son as the Mind, and the Holy Spirit as the Breath of God.
- I value Jesus Christ as the only Savior of fallen human beings, and the Lord-King of God's Kingdom.
- I value the Kingdom of God as the culture of the character of Heaven itself expressed in the created world, and the gracious rule and reign of the Lord Jesus

Christ within the creation that is rightly His, but temporarily occupied by the powers of darkness.

- I value God's great cosmic plan to reconcile all things to Himself.
- I value history as the arena for the advance of God's Kingdom all the way to total victory for His Kingdom and its rule in the world.
- I value the truth that there is no "secular" and "sacred," but all levels of history and human endeavor constitute the arena and field for the Kingdom and its advance in the world.
- I value the Book of Revelation as Spirit-given, a unique and treasured unveiling of the advance of God's Kingdom in the arena of history.
- I value *you,* as an image-bearer of God Himself, as one He desires to be blessed through the reading, study, and comprehension of the Book of Revelation, as a recipient of Christ's costly salvation, and a vital participant in His Kingdom advance.

My mission here is to present major themes of Revelation 12 in the context of history—especially that of the 21st century, our times—without diminishing the transcendent quality and sacred mystery of the visions entrusted to John and conveyed to us.

Keys to understanding Revelation

Let's say you have a safety deposit box inside a bank vault. Inside the metal container secured behind the thick metal door, steel bars and three feet of concrete are the most valuable things you possess—priceless jewelry, and bonds worth millions of dollars.

At age 50 you decide you have enough stored away in the safety deposit box to live well the rest of your life. You want to pay off your mortgage and travel the world in style. To do that, you must convert some of the assets in the box secured in the vault into hard cash. Happily you go to the bank, where you are escorted into the vault by an officer, straight to your personal safety deposit box.

To get to your wealth requires two keys. The bank officer inserts the key held by the bank. Then, with eagerness, you place the key you hold into the slot, and stand back as the banker turns the keys simultaneously. She escorts you to a cubicle, and leaves you inside to sort through the treasures in the safety deposit box.

This process illustrates the way to unlock the treasures of the Book of Revelation. Think of the "vault" as the whole Bible. The "safety deposit box" is the Book of Revelation. But it cannot be opened without the two "keys."

One key that unlocks the truth-treasures of Revelation to our understanding is the Bible's disclosures about the nature of time. Every belief system, whether secular materialism or religious mysticism, develops a theory of time. Western thought tends to see time as strictly linear, moving from beginning to termination, from past to present to future. Oriental philosophies, influenced by Hinduism and other nirvana religions view time as cyclical, moving in an endlessly repeating circle rather than a straight line.

The Bible reveals the reality of time that is both linear and cyclical. This is not as impossible as it sounds. Think of a train moving along a track. There is linear progression toward the destination, but the train is carried along by the cyclical, repeating motion of the wheels.

To dig out the richness of time as revealed in the Bible, we must do a bit of spade-work, sifting through categories of words appearing in both Testaments. Immediately when we open the Bible we run smack-dab into one of those vital terms. *Bereshith,* the Hebrew name for Genesis, means "the start," or "beginning." Genesis 2:4 sums up the whole of the Book of Genesis, when it says, "This is the history of the heavens and the earth when they were created." The Hebrew word for "history" appearing here is *toledah,* which means "generations." Thus, Genesis is the historical account that measures and reports on the foundational generations of all humanity.

"Genesis," the English term, comes from the Greek word, *geneseos*, signifying "birth," "generation," or the history of origins. The emphasis is on events and circumstances that surround the foundational generations of the human family.

Therefore, through the lens of the Bible, history is *generational* experience moving in a progressive pattern, toward a purpose. History must go forward from past into present, and finally into the future because it's impossible to reverse directions, and go back into the past (unless some of the more exotic implications of string theory, an idea regarding the physical construction of the universe, are true).

Forward progression necessitates a track on which history can move, and that is the meaning of time. Maimonides, a 12th century Torah scholar, understood the connection between historic movement and time. Time is the outcome, he said, "consequent upon motion." Neither can exist without the other. "Motion does not exist except in time, and time cannot be conceived by the intellect except together with motion," Maimonides thought.

The 'train' of time

Time is therefore like a train moving in a linear direction from a point of origin to a "terminal," on wheels that *cycle* along the *linear* tracks. History is the sequence of events that repeat themselves in broad style in linear progression, and time is the medium in which the motion of history can occur.

We see this in both the Old and New Testaments—the Hebrew Bible and the Greek Bible. Both the Hebrew and

Greek Bibles have special words to convey the reality of linear-cyclical time. *Zemdna* is translated "time" in the Old Testament, as is *moed. Zemdna* means time only in the sense of duration, the ticking of the clock. *Moed* refers to "appointed times," those periods in which defining events and directional circumstances arise in the lives of people, their relationships, and institutions.

The richness emerges in the conjunction of the two Hebrew words. The *Moedim* are the Feasts of Israel that mark significant intersections in space and time between the nation and God. *Zemdna*-time's myriad of moments finally arrives at the *Moedim,* in which the Hebrews interact with God through observances by which they move beyond human time. *Passover* takes the Israelites back to the night in Egypt that secured their delivery. *Purim* is a spiritual trip back in the time of Esther, and her courageous acts by which the Hebrews were saved from the genocide planned for them by Haman. *Yom Kippur* reaches outside *zemdna*-time, and releases the grace of God within the era of Law. Grace is a constant in the eternal continuum, but will not appear in earth-time until the completion of Christ's work on the cross, and yet is manifest in the *moed* of Passover and Yom Kippur.

In fact, the coming of the Messiah and His fulfillment of the covenant promises within space-time is what makes the linkage of *zemdna* and *moed* extraordinary. All the rescue events in Israel's experience brought about by God's direct intervention from outside human time (*zemdna*) are "salvific," that is, they point to the salvation that is reality in the eternal continuum, the Kingdom of Heaven, but which is yet to come in earth-time.

The linkage of the Old and New Testaments is what makes the Bible. Therefore, it should not surprise us that the Greek language of the New Testament reflects the *zemdna-moed* motif. The parallel Greek word for *zemdna,* sequential time as experienced in the natural world, is *kronos.* Another Greek term, *kairos,* expresses the ideas carried in the Hebrew *moed.* In fact, the significance of the *Moedim,* the Feasts, is that they are prophetic, linking the *zemdna*-future with the overarching realities of Heaven's time continuum.

As the linkage of *zemdna-moed* in the Old Testament gives rise to the Feasts by which heavenly intervention in space-time is remembered, celebrated, and entered into once more, so there is linkage in the New Testament between *kairos* and *kronos.* This junction of the two qualities of time is expressed in the New Testament by the term, "the fullness of time." In the Old, the arrival in the chronological calendar of the *Moedim,* constituted the "fullness of time." In the New Testament, the arrival in chronological time of the reality to which the Feasts of Israel pointed is the "fullness of time."

Now the imagery is different. "Fullness" is from the Greek word, *pleroma,* which is seen graphically in the filling of a cup to the rim. Chronological time drips in seconds, minutes, hours, days, weeks, months, and years, until the cup of history reaches a degree of fullness.

One Destination

Every event celebrated in the Old Testament looked forward to one thing—the Coming of the Messiah. Therefore, Paul writes, in Galatians 4:4, that "when the fullness of the time came, God sent forth His Son, born of a woman, born under the Law." The Son exists eternally with the Father, and is therefore a remarkable *kairos*-Person who becomes incarnate in *kronos*-sequence. He is literally a Being from another dimension!

When He appears in chronological order, He fulfills all creation history to that point. When He comes again, He will fulfill all of history from the time of the Resurrection and Ascension to the point of His Second Coming.

One of the keys, therefore, that helps unlock the understanding of the Revelation visions is the awareness John is seeing and, through the Holy Spirit, conveying to us, the *moed-kairos* actualities within *zemdna-kronos*. If we view them only on the flat plane of one time-dimension, they make no sense.

This is a major problem with the primary approaches to interpreting Revelation. They are all one-dimensional in their concept of time, seeing Revelation only within *kronos*-time.

They each try to interpret Revelation within that limited time-perspective.

- *Preterists* believe all the events depicted in Revelation were fulfilled in the past, during the persecution of the Church in ancient Rome, and in the destruction of Jerusalem in 70 AD.
- *Futurists* believe Revelation is pointing to things that will only occur out ahead in time.
- *Historicists* are perhaps more one-dimensional than any of the others. Some isolate the meaning of the Revelation visions around the rise of the Roman Catholic Church and the papacy.
- *Idealists* see Revelation's visions as perhaps not having substance within *kronos*-time at all, but are mostly symbolic representations of divine truth, like an impressionist painting.

However, the events revealed in Revelation do occur in space-time. They are historic realities that repeat in general, if not specific, form all across the linear track. However, they are culminating to major, consummating events. Therefore, "many tribulations" across *kronos*-history culminate in the *Mega*-Tribulation. "Many antichrists" are finally summed up in the Antichrist. Numerous outpourings of judgments in the form of having to endure the consequences of sinful deeds ultimately add up to the Great White Throne Judgment.

The understanding of time as linear-cyclical provides clarity for other issues, like the Babylon-Rome cycle. Both images arise in the Book of Revelation, and seem to be the same entity. In a large sense, they are. Babylon is the symbol of the world system attempting to organize itself without, and, in many cases, in defiance of God. The reason Babylon is chosen by the Holy Spirit as the prime expression of the anti-God world system is because of its founder, Nimrod. Genesis 10:8 describes him as a "mighty one on the earth." Nimrod is the first radical humanist, a man whose arrogance swells to the point he sees himself as his only necessity. He builds cities and a kingdom that does not acknowledge God, laying the foundations of the world system. Rome someday will be another manifestation of society birthed from Nimrod's spiritual DNA, as will Greece, Persia, and all human empires. The Book of Daniel, as well as Revelation, shows these manifestations cycling along the *zemdna/kronos*-track, speeding toward their consummate forms, unveiled in the Book of Revelation.

Revelation is not about symbolic fantasies, but the reality that explodes into space-time as *zemdna-moed/kronos-kairos* come together like colliding galaxies. This is Jesus' point in Matthew 24. In that stunningly apocalyptic passage, He says, "many will come in My name, saying, 'I am the Christ,' and will mislead many. You will be hearing of wars and rumors of wars. See that you are not frightened, for *those things* must take place, but *that* is not yet the end. For nation will rise against nation, and kingdom against kingdom, and in various places there will be famines and earthquakes. But all these things are *merely* the beginning of birth pangs... the coming of the Son of Man will be just like the days of Noah. For as in those days before the flood they were eating and drinking, marrying and giving in marriage, until the day that Noah entered the ark, and they did not understand until the flood came and took them all away; so will the coming of the Son of Man be. (Matthew 24:6-8, 37-39, italics in original)

Zemdna-kronos events will be cycling over and again on the linear track, when suddenly *moed-kairos* intervenes in space-time. All the history since Christ's Ascension will have reached its fullness!

Matthew 24 also brings us to the second key that will unlock the Book of Revelation—the Kingdom of God. This, more than anything else, is the theme of the visions unveiled to John. In fact, the Messiah and His Kingdom are what the whole Bible is about.

The Book of Revelation shows the dynamics of two phenomena within the linear-cyclical duality of time. One is the progression of God's Kingdom within a world in a state of decline under the power of the evil one. (1 John 5:19) The ultimate outcome of the regressive plunge is Hell. The progression of the Kingdom brings the redeemed world to the ultimate of its restoration as Paradise, the steady-state of the Kingdom of Heaven.

The Book of Revelation cannot be understood apart from the Kingdom of God, its "seeding" and advance in the world. If we look behind the "curtain," it is the grand battle for and ultimate victory of the Kingdom of God that we see!

'Curtains'

I confess to being a *film noir* fan. I love the black-and-white mystery cinema of the 1940s and 1950s. Your brain has to do most of the work because the plot-lines, like the visuals, build on subtlety, shadowy inference, innuendo, and nuance. I especially enjoy *noir*-speech. When a gravelly *film noir* villain says, "It's curtains for you!" he means the victim is done for.

Film noir is impossible in today's tech-driven cinema. Audiences are accustomed to everything being done for them. The imagination rarely has to kick in. Sex and gore are anything but subtle. Intricate plots cannot be woven in movies whose scenes must flash at a bewildering velocity, and where the only double *entendre* contemporary viewers might grasp deal with sex. Nevertheless, we've held on to the expression, "Curtains!" Its implications are almost always sinister. The curtain is dropping, bringing doom and the end.

The actual title of the Book of Revelation in the Greek original is *Apocalupsis* ("Apocalypse"). This word refers to an "uncovering" of something that has been hidden. Strangely, interpreters and popular opinion mostly see *Apocalupsis* in the *film noir* sense of gloom and doom. Yes, the curtain is coming down on *zemdna-kronos* time and all the phenomena trapped within it, like the world system, but that's not the heart and soul of the Book of Revelation. The lifting of the curtain is the throbbing passion of Revelation.

Speaking of old movies, "The Great Ziegfeld," a 1936 filmography of famous impresario Flo Ziegfeld, contains one of the most spectacular curtain-raising scenes in cinema history. To the tune of "A Pretty Girl Is Like a Melody," 4,300 yards of silk rayon curtain lift on a towering and rotating wedding cake festooned with 180 cast members, a grand piano, and a spectacularly gowned actress at the top. The massive curtain is segmented, and each portion opens to reveal the next view of the "wedding cake" as it rotates into view. The audience watches eagerly for the ascent of each segment of the curtain to see what's behind.

To look at the unveilings of *The Apocalypse* with dread is as contradictory as the audience watching the Ziegfeld movie sequence awaiting the lifting of the curtain on each tier of the spectacular set with foreboding. Yes, *The Apocalypse* has some scary elements, but the raising of the curtain reveals the thrilling story of the advance of God's Kingdom on the stage of history!

The imagery appears throughout the New Testament. "It is finished!" declared Jesus, at the end of His ordeal on the cross. This wasn't a weak-voiced concession to defeat. *Tetelestai* is the Greek term. It means the completion of a mission, the accomplishment of a mission, the fulfilling of a vision. Jesus was announcing that He had succeeded in the goal for which He came into the world—establishing through His atonement the means of all things being reconciled to God. At that moment, the hefty curtain separating the Holy of Holies from the rest of the Temple compound was split. The curtain is removed; the way to God is now completely open through Christ's work.

As Jesus ascended to the Father, He became our "forerunner" through the veil of Heaven itself. (Hebrews 6:19-20) Now we "have confidence to enter the holy place by the blood of Jesus, by a new and living way which He inaugurated for us through the veil, that is, His flesh," says Hebrews 10:19-20.

The Book of Revelation is therefore a collection of visions the Lord gives the Apostle John that allowed him to see the lifting of the curtain and the advance of God's Kingdom across the stage of history. In line with the biblical teaching about the nature of time, John sees events that cycle in broad form, repeating in linear progression from one end of the stage to the other.

Getting inside John's visions

This book is not a commentary on Revelation 12. For one thing I am not worthy to stand with the scholars and expositors who have written exhaustively on Revelation. And that's another reason I am not writing a commentary: there are enough of those to fill the Library of Congress.

Instead, we will seek in these pages to get inside old John's vision, tremble with him, fall in awe alongside him, rejoice with him. We will attempt to "come up here" with the veteran Apostle, and see with him what he sees.

I don't believe in trying to reduce the rich substance of Scripture into a mere narrative that gives us the big picture without the detail. But I will try to convey the transcendent and mystical quality of the visions given the Apostle John.

To set the stage on which the curtain will lift, and upon which the scenes will be unveiled, we must go all the way back to the beginning—and beyond. As we do, we will see that the epic we are about to behold in the Book of Revelation is a magnificent love story!

In interpreting the Revelation—and all the rest of the Bible's apocalyptic literature—to get bogged down in speculative detail is to lose the perspective of the Big Picture.

Special Note:
Revelation and Hermeneutic
(Interpretive) Method

Sometimes to see things as they really are we have to get far above them. The big picture is clearest from altitude.

I remember a remarkable night in the late 1970s, not long after the jumbo jet, the Boeing 747, debuted. I had to connect in Atlanta to a westbound flight. It was a 747 being "repositioned," which meant among other things there were only 18 passengers served by a crew of about twice that number.

We took off after dark, and started a run over the Deep South at more than 30,000 feet. But in the unusual clarity of that moonless night, at that altitude we saw a much bigger picture to the north than could ever be visible that far south.

Over Louisiana, the pilot told us that if we looked out the right-side windows we could see the Aurora Borealis, the shimmering dance of light normally spotted in more northerly regions. Down in the Deep South we earthbound folk never even think of looking for the Aurora Borealis. It doesn't exist for us.

But get way up high on a cloudless, mistless, fogless night and you can see the big picture—what is really "there" even if it's not "there" over Dixie.

That's the meaning of the whole Bible. The Holy Spirit, projecting the Biggest of pictures through the personalities of human writers, lifts us way up high. At such an altitude we can actually stand above earth-time (kronos, relative time, finite time), and see it from start to finish.

For example, the Book of Revelation is possible because of what is described in Revelation 4:1, where John reports that "(a)fter these things I looked, and behold, a door standing open in heaven, and the first voice which I had heard, like the sound of a trumpet speaking with me, said, 'Come up here, and I will show you what must take place after these things.'" NASU

John goes to the ultimate "up there" and can see the whole of salvation history laid out beneath Him.

Our problem in interpreting the Book of Revelation is that we too often try to understand it from "down here" rather than from "up there." That's like an ant trying to figure out the whole human by generalizing from the tiny cluster of mass making up the person's shoe-sole, which is all the empirical data the ant can gather from its perspective.

Danger of getting 'bogged down'

In interpreting the Revelation—and all the rest of the Bible's apocalyptic literature—to get bogged down in speculative detail is to lose the perspective of the Big Picture.

For example, every interpretive system has its own ideas about the meaning of the designation "1,260 days" that appears both in Daniel and Revelation. All the hermeneutic schemes have their own theories of "7 years", "1,000 years", "70 weeks", and much more.

It's easy to get mired in that swamp of speculation, and miss the Big Picture. Edward Irving was among the founders in 1832 of the Catholic Apostolic Church. He wrote an impressive commentary on the Hebrew Text of Daniel's prophecies. But he was way too far "down here" and was seriously misled. Irving declared that Daniel's visions referred to Napoleon Bonaparte, that Britain was God's "faithful witness," and that Louis XVI even made an appearance.

In our own times of course, there has been Hal Lindsay's *The Late Great Planet Earth.* There he said the 10 horns of the beast in both Daniel and Revelation was the European Common Market. There were only six member states when he wrote, but Lindsay covered that by saying eventually there would be 10. However, there would actually be as many as 15. 1980, wrote Lindsay from his "down here" perspective in 1970, would likely be the climax of history.[1] Here's how we know that conclusions about the detailed meaning tends to be speculative: Every time someone asks, "Wallace, Tim LaHaye says the seventy weeks of Daniel are actually clusters of seven years, totaling 490 years... What's your view?"

What is being asked is that I speculate on LaHaye's (or whoever's) speculation. I won't go there. The reason is that I like the Bible to say what it says, not what I or anyone else, or an interpretive system speculates is what it says.

If I am not ready to camp out on the speculative detail, I am definitely going to build on the deep foundation of non-speculative, established absolute truth. It's not that I am suggesting the detail itself is mere speculation, because the Bible is historically and factually true in everything it presents. What I am saying is that speculative interpretations of the actual details become the "truth" about the detail, even though they may miss it by a galaxy or so.

Nothing shows this more clearly than the unfortunate allegorical preaching that characterized many Medieval (and later) pulpits. Some Bible books are intended to be taken as allegory—Song of Solomon, for example, or when Peter uses the Old Testament historic event of Noah's Ark and the Flood as an allegory of New Testament salvation (1 Peter 3:20-22).

---

[1] Both these examples were taken from John Stott, *The Incomparable Christ.*

But when preachers and commentators try to interpret all the Bible allegorically, serious distortion occurs, winding up in twisted doctrine at best or heresy at worst.

This is why I avoid saying specifically what the 1,260 days of Daniel and Revelation signify. What we do know is that this is

1. A period of determined length
2. Therefore an event headed toward some specific conclusion
3. Determination and conclusion mean God's purpose is at work, and that the events so stipulated are part of that great purpose

Applied to Revelation 12:

1. There will be a specific period of kronos-time when Israel will be protected from the dragon

This is "cosmic Israel," the Israel that always exists in the Mind of God as His Covenant people, crucial to His cosmic plan, and which will be manifest as a racial and geopolitical entity at certain points along the sequential history of kronos-time. When Jesus appears with implementation of God's cosmic (kairological) plan in kronos-time and finite space, it is now possible for the non-Jew to be brought into the "cosmic Israel." The dragon turns from the "woman" and focuses on this larger Israel, which, as we will see, has protection for a specified period as well.

This cosmic Israel is in view when Jesus tells the Jewish religious leaders who have rejected Him that He was removing from them the privilege of being the agents for the continuation of the promise to Abraham that his seed would bring blessing to the whole world. Specifically, says Jesus, in Matthew 21:43, "the kingdom of God will be taken away from you and given to a people, producing the fruit of it."

This is also the topic in Rom 9:6-9, where Paul writes that

> not everyone born into a Jewish family is truly a Jew! Just the fact that they are descendants of Abraham doesn't make them truly Abraham's children. For the Scriptures say, "Isaac is the son through whom your descendants will be counted," though Abraham had other children, too. This means that Abraham's physical descendants are not necessarily children of God. It is the children of the promise who are considered to be Abraham's children. (NLT)

Under the Holy Spirit's inspiration, the Apostle continues on the theme of the larger "cosmic" Israel in Romans 11:11-18:

> Did God's people stumble and fall beyond recovery? Of course not! His purpose was to

make his salvation available to the Gentiles, and then the Jews would be jealous and want it for themselves. Now if the Gentiles were enriched because the Jews turned down God's offer of salvation, think how much greater a blessing the world will share when the Jews finally accept it. I am saying all of this especially for you Gentiles. God has appointed me as the apostle to the Gentiles. I lay great stress on this, for I want to find a way to make the Jews want what you Gentiles have, and in that way I might save some of them. For since the Jews' rejection meant that God offered salvation to the rest of the world, how much more wonderful their acceptance will be. It will be life for those who were dead! And since Abraham and the other patriarchs were holy, their children will also be holy. For if the roots of the tree are holy, the branches will be, too. But some of these branches from Abraham's tree, some of the Jews, have been broken off. And you Gentiles, who were branches from a wild olive tree, were grafted in. So now you also receive the blessing God has promised Abraham and his children, sharing in God's rich nourishment of his special olive tree. But you must be careful not to brag about being grafted in to replace the branches that were broken off. Remember, you are just a branch, not the root. (NLT)

2. The appearance of the cosmic Israel (the Israel consisting of both believing Jews and Gentiles) and the season of its protection is part of the kronos-sequence leading to the specific conclusion ordained by God.
3. The events and hard-to-discern details are part of the Grand Purpose of God, which is that the Kingdom of God will rule in a world where all things are reconciled to the Father, and restored to the mint condition of Eden prior to the Fall.

This is summed up in Jesus's statement in Matthew 24:14 about the purpose of all history, including that of both cosmic and historic Israel: "This gospel of the kingdom shall be preached in the whole world as a testimony to all the nations, and then the end (*telos,* purpose) will come."

Therefore the Bible discourages us from making prophetic calendars and this explains why God will not permit us to know the day and hour of Christ's return. If we do, we will get bogged down in the swamp of the "down here" and miss the Big Picture of Jesus, His Kingdom, and His Coming, seen from "up there."

It's not that the details are unimportant, and some of the projections and speculations are undoubtedly true. But the greater concern of the whole Bible is that we see the Big Picture and don't spend all our time detouring around speculative notions.

Again, here's the Big Picture, what we know for certain without the help or necessity of human speculation:

- God has a vast cosmic plan for the redemption of the world and restoration to its original mint condition
- Jesus Christ has accomplished all necessary for the execution of this plan
- The powers of darkness resist it passionately because it leads ultimately to their eternity in the lake of fire
- We are living in the End Times that began with the Resurrection and Ascension of Jesus
- The cosmic war in the heavens intensifies and spills over into our dimension, with sometimes catastrophic effects
- But all this is part of the Great Plan that will culminate in the Coming again of Jesus the Christ, and the establishment of His Kingdom in the world.

Lucifer's idolizing of himself becomes the malignancy that will metastasize into all false worship. The idolization of the self is the seed of all idolatry. The false gods will always be formed in the images arising from the heart and mind of their creators, just as the True springs from the Heart and Mind of the *I Am*, and is formed by His Breath.

PROLOGUE:
LOVE STORY
BEFORE THERE IS WAR THERE IS LOVE.

The All arises from the Heart of the One. *I Am* experiences the individual components of the All, then thinks it, then speaks it, and it is. Speaking is the expulsion of breath, and Zoe-life is propelled into the Continuum. *I Am* breathes, and the passion in the Heart of the One, which forms the thought in the Mind of the One, and the expression of the thought through the Mouth of the One takes on existence in the Boundless-Timeless Domain, over which the One is King.

But the One is not solitary. The Heart is Father, the Mind is Son, and the Breath is the Spirit. Heart, mind, and breath are different, each a Person, yet one, a tri-unity.

Out of the Continuum comes the Cosmos.

The infinite Being creates an arena of space. In the beginning, the space-time Cosmos is an extension of the Boundless-Timeless. There is no barrier between the Dimensions of the All. The beings in each move back and forth. The root-runners of Paradise sprout with beauty in both Dimensions. The Cosmos is theater-in-the-round, and in the center is a vast, uncurtained stage. Some of the inhabitants of the Continuum are selected to walk the boards of space and time. They are costumed in forms that can exist and function in the arena of existence in space-time.

The play is an epic.

The theme is love.

Before the Beginning

Before the space-time Cosmos its beings frolic in an ocean of uninterrupted goodness, peace, and joy, arising in the Heart of the *I Am,* conceived in the Mind of the *I Am,* brought into manifest form by the Breath of the *I Am.* Pure Being, flawless, pristine in motive, singular in character dreams of Beings like Himself, and all His dreams become manifest. His thoughts are so numerous the Boundless-Timeless Realm has a population that cannot be numbered.

The beings arising from *The* Being have never experienced the narrowing, fragmentation, and stratification of time. They experience no boredom, do not fret with anxiety, do not wince at memories past. There is no future to fear, no past to regret, no present as a medium for tedium. There is only Being singing songs that never become old, tasting joy that never hardens into staleness, dancing with energy that never fades.

The populace of the eternal Continuum, like a solar system, twirl in ecstasy around the glorious Radiance enthroned at the center. The gravitational force that holds the Boundless-Timeless Realm together is love. It is the strong force, the binding dynamic of all that is in the Dominion of the *I Am.*

Love is expansive. Lovers are always seeking new vessels into which they can pour their bounty of goodness, peace, and joy. Lovers must have counterparts to themselves who can receive and give love. This is the amplification of love.

It is also the risk and grief of love. *I Am* is not a machine, and the recipients of His love must not be machines. The deep mystery of the eternal Continuum is why *I Am* chose love as the nature and motivation of His Heart. *I Am* is all-sufficient, uncreated, perfectly free to choose whatever will be the passion driving His boundless energy.

Therefore, all the beings arising in His Mind are experienced first in His Heart. The *I Am* feels love at the Core of His Being, then, in His Mind, dresses the passion in form that can feel what He feels. What the *I Am* feels in His Heart and forms in His Mind, He speaks into existence. He calls forth the something out of the nothing. Speech is the expulsion of breath. All who come from the Heart and Mind of *I Am* are His out-breathings.

The risk and grief lie in the fact that to receive His love created beings must have compatibility with His Being. They must be like Him. They must be free. He therefore thinks of them as receiving and responding to His love, but the *I Am* must permit a place in His Mind to allow his created ones to say No to His offer of love. Otherwise the love is not authentic.

Why Lucifer

The first to say No is the most beautiful of the Heart-Mind-Breath creations of the *I Am*. Lucifer, Star of the Morning, bright and shining one, the leader of praise, the perfumed scent and atmosphere of the Continuum. Worship is the return of love to the *I Am* by the beings conceived in His Heart, gestated in His Mind, and born from the womb of His Breath-propelled Speech. Lucifer has the high honor of conducting the vast chorale of adoration, the harmonics of Heaven, the melody shaped by transcendent mathematics that will ultimately form all cosmic order, the music of the spheres.

Not even the *I Am* permits Himself to be the sole recipient of His own love. True love demands otherness, or it deteriorates into a warped adoration of self. If *I Am* loves only Himself then He brings into manifest reality beings He can despise, dominate, and torture as objects of the opposite of love—hate.

But now Lucifer introduces a new theme into the epic, that of self-limited love. This is the leaven that corrupts, that will poison the passion of the Continuum. The elevation of self-love within Lucifer's heart means the dividing of his own being. Rather than pure love for the *I Am* and Lucifer's love for himself united in the intimacy of the tri-unity of the *I Am,* there is now a competing affection. Lucifer's love for himself outpaces his love of *I Am* and his participation and delight in that authentic love. A part of himself is at war with another part of himself. Rather than wholeness of love, Lucifer is now a disintegrated being. Lucifer's infection has already begun spreading through the eternal Continuum's freedom, and will ultimately distort and sicken the love in a third of the inhabitants of the Boundless-Timeless Domain.

Lucifer's idolizing of himself becomes the malignancy that will metastasize into all false worship. The idolization of the self is the seed of all idolatry. The false gods will always be formed in the images arising from the heart and mind of their creators, just as the True springs from the Heart and Mind of the *I Am,* and is formed by His Breath.

Lucifer cannot remain at the Throne of the Most High.

The *Outside*

The glorious angel is expelled from the Boundless-Timeless Continuum. But where will he go? *Outside.* But where and what is "outside"? If the Star of the Morning can no longer dwell in the Boundless-Timeless Continuum, then he must exist in the bounded-tensed discontinuity. But All is encompassed in the Boundless-Timeless Domain, and there is nothing outside it. Therefore, if the *I Am's* love is authentic, and will permit the possibilities that freedom demands, *I Am* must allow the bounded-tensed discontinuity to come into being. It will be the Outside where Lucifer will establish his rule. *Ouranos* ("sky," "heaven") is the seat of thrones. Thus

Lucifer's passage from the Continuum creates the non-contiguous *ouranos*. His movement from the Infinite brings into reality the finite—the Second *Ouranos,* the Second Heaven.

Ultimately what was once the All will be a three-tiered construct, with *I Am's* image-bearers having His dominion in the First Heaven, Lucifer ruling in the Second Heaven, and *I Am* enthroned in the highest, the Third Heaven. But the authority for the thrones of the Second Heaven come either from *I Am's* permissive will—that of the Second Heaven—or the intentional will of *I Am*—that of the First Heaven. Ultimately the Throne of *I Am* and all that conforms to it is all that will be left. But that gets ahead of the storyline of the grand drama whose theme is love.

Lucifer's expulsion from *inside* the Continuum forms the *outside.*

The Continuum is Cosmos—peace and harmonic order founded upon and sustained by love. But the Outside is chaos, the distortion of love, the rule of hate, the perversion of every good thing that comes from the Heart-Mind of I Am.

If *I Am's* Domain is the Continuum of Boundless-Timeless Cosmos, then the Outside, which is the result of Lucifer's plummet, is not a continuum, but a discontinuous fragmentation into chunks of space and segments of time. Up and down become a problem. Past raises impenetrable walls. Present becomes such a fleeting interval some who will experience it will conclude it is a mere fantasy. Future will loom and stir anxiety in those who must inhabit the fragmented realm.

In the Outside, speech, once the glistening jewel on the great tree of Logos, is smashed into heaps of shards. Words cut and wound. Once all speech arose from the Mind of *I Am,* and centered on the wonder and glory of *I Am* and His truth. Speech had meaning and purpose and beauty. But in the Outside, the edge of speech is a sharpened razor. Speech is the point of a stabbing sword. In the Outside speech does not *express* meaning so much as it *searches* for meaning. Truth-spinners and speech-writers will quest for the right word to veil truth and meaning, not expose it. This is because Lucifer is the father of lies. The Continuum is the domain of pure Logos. The Outside is the realm of deceit. Therefore the eternal Continuum is the Kingdom of Light, and the Outside is the kingdom of darkness.

I Am's relentless love

However, *I Am* is relentless in His love. His desire is to extend His love even into the core of the Outside. *I Am* will carve out of the formlessness and barrenness a wonderful Paradise, whose loveliness is created through its unbroken unity between the Kingdom of Light and the heart of the Outside.

Therefore, *I Am* envisions the universe in His Mind, speaks the creative Logos-Word, and suddenly it is there. The Spirit hovers over the nest of creation, nurturing into space-time existence all the thought-components of *I Am's* Mind, spoken into being in His Logos. In the midst of it all, *I Am* plants the Garden that will be the Place of the local manifestation of Himself, the Omnipresent One, for the sake of interaction with those who will carry His image into this new world of space-time. In the future, which is an element of the new category of time, this localization will be in the Temple, and ultimately in the Logos, Who will take human form. But in the beginning the Garden is the realm of *I Am's* localization of Himself. He will walk in the Garden and that is why the Garden will be Paradise.

I Am will place beings in this Paradise who will be structured to exist in the physics of the Outside, and yet have His life-nature—Zoe—as their life-energy. These beings will be *Imago Dei,* made in the image of *I Am.* They will be multi-dimensional, capable of crossing the bridge connecting the Continuum—the Kingdom of Light—and the Paradise at the heart of the Outside. The bridge will span the vast abyss, which is the kingdom of darkness. Above all, the *Imago Dei* will be capable of receiving the love *I Am* is determined to share with all who will open themselves to it.

But once again that introduces risk and grief. Bondage is the cruel style of the kingdom of darkness, but freedom is the dynamic allowed to flourish in the Paradise in the heart of the Outside. Love is no more possible there without freedom than it is in the Continuum.

For age upon age, the *Imago Dei* beings in Paradise luxuriate in loving, intimate relationship with *I Am*. As they are formed in His image, so He appears to them in Paradise in the imagery of the world over which He has granted them regency. He crosses over to them, and they can cross over to Him. He fellowships with them in the Garden, and they enjoy the life-quality of the Kingdom of Light.

They are one in relationship with Him, one in relationship with their selves, one in relationship with each other, and one in relationship with nature. That grandly tiered unity is the beauty, peace, and joy of Paradise. The harmonics have expressed themselves as the music of the spheres, and it is the melody the *Imago Dei* beings—Adam and Eve—sing, and the tune to which they dance.

I Am's relentless, expansive love fills everything. There is no predator-mindedness, no idolatrous self-assertiveness that drives one to seek mastery over another, no slithering desire to exploit and dominate and control.

Until the serpent slinks in.

The disintegrated being becomes the catalyst of fragmentation. Lucifer will make for himself a rival realm. However, the art exists first in the mind of the artist. Lucifer's fragmented soul gives rise to the twisted kingdom, a vast waste of ruin.

Evil, and the sin it conceives is a disruption of the continuity of relationship.

- First the disruption of the *Imago Dei* from relationship with the *I Am.*

- Second, the fragmentation of the self of the *Imago Dei*, in which there is now a part of the *Imago Dei* that wants to love and follow Lucifer, even while a portion of the *Imago Dei* wants to hold on to affection for *I Am.* This means the *Imago Dei* now has within his and her soul something also of the image of shattered Lucifer. For the first time Adam feels shame, and is compelled to hide himself. He is the same being who once felt so secure he was unconscious of his nakedness before *I Am,* and felt safe in his exposure.

- Third in the sundering of relationships through evil is the dividing of human relationship. For the first time Adam sees the nakedness of Eve and realizes she is *not-Adam*, but other, not in the sense of the other who can receive his love, but the other who is a competitor and even adversary. In oneness, they experienced their identity of *Imago Dei* in male-female form. But now that they are sundered, who bears the *Imago Dei?* Adam will conclude Eve is something less than himself, and Eve will see Adam sometimes as not the *Imago Dei,* but the image of the beast.

- Fourth, cut from *I Am,* fragmented in soul and spirit, sundered from one another, the *Imago Dei* is severed from relationship with nature, and becomes the enemy and exploiter of creation.

But is the Fragmented Realm to be all there is? The *I Am* and His mighty love cannot permit it to be so! *Out of the Continuum comes the cosmos.* There will be two stages in the arena of the Outside—one in which *I Am's* love has been absolutely and finally rejected, and one in which *I Am's* love is still a possibility. When Lucifer rejected *I Am's* love he also rejected freedom. But in this new Ouranos freedom will still exist, because this is the only way *I Am's* love can be *possible.*

On a certain Sunday morning

Kronos comes into existence. And on one of its days, a Sunday morning, an old man existing in the Fragmented Realm is taken "in the spirit" and permitted to see the eternal Continuum and the view of the Fragmented Realm from the perspective of *I Am* Himself. The gaunt saint looks down from *I Am's* lofty position and sees the interactions of the Eternal and the tensed, the Infinite and the finite. As he watches, the curtain begins to descend on one of the stages, and the curtain on the other begins to rise.

With immense shock and awe, John beholds the mystery behind the great veil that has concealed the view of the Continuum from those whose eyes can only see the Fragmented Realm.

The kronos-weary man beholds *Apocalupsis*—the raising of the curtain behind which is the I Am, the eternal Continuum, and the Great Epic of Love!

Chapter 1

'COME UP HERE!'

At the moment as I write there are some new dynamics that have come into the continuing powder keg of the Middle East that could have an explosive effect. Most of us have never known a time when the Middle East was not headline news. Now the region is more unstable than ever.

The new elements are as destabilizing as someone using nitroglycerin bottles as bowling pins. The alignments and portents are not a surprise to those who view the world through the lens of the Bible. Never in history have those alignments been closer to the patterns revealed in the Bible's prophetic literature than now.

Specifically:

- The Shiite 12th Imam doctrine has never been as influential nor had a greater platform than now. Iran's highest leader, Imam Kahmeini, believes he has a mandate to precipitate the arrival of the 12th Imam. This will happen through, among other things, an all-out assault on Israel.

- The Syria conflict has revealed a triangular set of relationships in the alignment of nations foreshadowing prophecies in Ezekiel. Russia, the great power to the north, is aligning with Iran, which is supporting Assad in Syria.

- The United States, the protector of the State of Israel since its founding in 1948, is fading as a significant player. The President of the United States either has no comprehensive foreign policy vision, and therefore no cogent strategy, or he actually tilts toward Al Qaeda and the Muslim Brotherhood, Sunni Muslims fighting Shiite Muslims in the form of Assad and Iran.

The big questions are: What is driving the specific global situation now (it is global because a widespread war in the Middle East would seriously disrupt the energy sector, with huge impact on the global economy)? Second: What has driven this rage across history?

Is it possible that what we experience in the natural dimension we presently inhabit is the "spillover" of the larger war in the transnatural dimension—the "heavens"—spoken of in Revelation 12?

That will be our focus in these studies. We will examine the new dynamics that have entered the Middle East fray in the light of biblical revelation. We will also seek to understand the "spillover effect" on our personal lives, families, and other spheres of engagement.

First, let's review the vital contextual background of the Book of Revelation in general and Revelation 12 specifically.

The Book of Revelation generally:

1. The Revelation centers on Jesus Christ and His Kingdom advance in this world.

2. Neither Israel, nor the United States, nor any other human nation is the focus of Revelation. The geopolitical nations are "bit players" essential to the drama, but not the topic of the drama.

3. The "nation" that plays a central role in Revelation is the "Church." The "nation" identity of the authentic Church is made clear in Revelation 1:6 ("He has made us to be a kingdom, priests to His God and Father ..." NASU) and Revelation 5:10 ("You have made them to be a kingdom and priests to our God; and they will reign upon the earth." NASU).

4. A vital hermeneutic key for interpreting Revelation is the biblically revealed nature of time, disclosed in the Hebrew words translated "time" and their Greek cognates.

The greatest mistake many make in interpreting Revelation is not knowing or forgetting what the Bible reveals about the nature of time, as we have seen above. The biblical view of time straightens out much confusion in the interpretation of the Book of Revelation—as well as all prophetic and apocalyptic literature in the Bible.

In Old Testament Hebrew, actions are focused on content and completion, not by the process leading to completion over past, present, and future. Both "past" and "future" in the biblical understanding of time are existent. The past is the "before" reality, and the future is "there" in *mow-ed-kairos* time, but we just haven't arrived there yet.

If you get on a train headed to New York in Central Standard Time, New York is already existent in Eastern Standard Time, which you have not yet entered. You don't make it come into existence by traveling to it. Therefore, the "future" is already a reality toward which we are moving.

Not only does the understanding of time clear up some of the tough passages in Revelation, but also in Genesis. For example, since Hebrew "time" focuses on completion, and not process in past-present-future, this means the six days of creation are declared at the conclusion of whatever sequence is involved leading to the *telos*, or purpose of that "day." It may have taken a billion years or it may have taken 24 hours for God to declare the completion of "Day 1."

"Time" for us is quantitative, the number of minutes in an hour, the number of hours in a day, and so on. The numbers exist in the kronos-nature of time revealed in the Bible, but *the primary focus of biblically revealed time is qualitative, not quantitative.* That is, the Bible zeroes in on the content of time rather than the quantitative numbering that adds up to a sequence.

So, rather than focusing on "when" sequentially the Revelation trumpet-judgments are sounded, or "when" there was-is-will be "war in heaven" our attention must be given to the impact of the event whatever its time-construct.

With all that in mind, let's take a general look at Revelation 12.

A Journey into the *Kairological* Realm

What has happened to John as he receives the Revelation visions is this: He has been brought by the Holy Spirit into *kairos*-time. John is still very much in *kronos*-time. He tells us that specifically in Revelation 1:9-13:

> I, John, your brother and fellow partaker in the tribulation and kingdom and perseverance which are in Jesus, was on the island called Patmos because of the word of God and the testimony of Jesus. I was in the Spirit on the Lord's Day, and I heard behind me a loud voice like the sound of a trumpet, saying, " Write in a book what you see, and send it to the seven churches: to Ephesus and to Smyrna and to Pergamum and to Thyatira and to Sardis and to Philadelphia and to Laodicea." Then I turned to see the voice that was speaking with me. And having turned I saw seven golden lampstands; and in the middle of the lampstands I saw one like a son of man, clothed in a robe reaching to

the feet, and girded across His chest with a golden sash.

"The Lord's Day" is *kronos*-specific, the first day of the week, but is *kairos*-focused. What makes the *kronos*-day special is the *kairos* that was both outside and inside *kronos* (*kairos* has the capacity of intervening in *kronos*; the means by which *kronos* can cross over into *kairos* is through prayer, praise and worship.) But the *kairos* that makes the *kronos* of the first day significant is the Atonement and Resurrection of Jesus Christ. We know this is a *kairotic* event because Revelation 13:8 says this of Jesus:

> And all that dwell upon the earth shall worship him, whose names are not written in the book of life of the Lamb slain from the foundation of the world...

Back in Revelation 1, John goes on to say,

> "Then I turned to see the voice that was speaking with me. And having turned I saw seven golden lampstands; and in the middle of the lampstands I saw one like a son of man, clothed in a robe reaching to the feet, and girded across His chest with a golden sash."

John "turns" in the *kronos* moment, and immediately sees what is happening in the *kairos* realm.

Revelation 4 gives us an even more graphic sense of what John experienced in this movement between *kronos* and *kairos*:

> After these things I looked, and behold, a door standing open in heaven, and the first voice which I had heard, like the sound of a trumpet speaking with me, said, "Come up here, and I will show you what must take place after these things." Immediately I was in the Spirit; and behold, a throne was standing in heaven, and One sitting on the throne.

"Come up here" in Greek does not only refer to a spatial, or quantitative movement, but also a qualitative ascent. That is, John is invited to rise up into another level of time, that of the Kingdom of Heaven. This can only happen "in the Spirit."

The Holy Spirit, through Paul, gives us a deeper understanding of this, in 1 Corinthians 2:12-16:

> Now we have received, not the spirit of the world, but the Spirit who is from God, so that we may know the things freely given to us by God, which things we also speak, not in words taught

55

by human wisdom, but in those taught by the Spirit, combining spiritual thoughts with spiritual words. But a natural man does not accept the things of the Spirit of God, for they are foolishness to him; and he cannot understand them, because they are spiritually appraised. But he who is spiritual appraises all things, yet he himself is appraised by no one. For WHO HAS KNOWN THE MIND OF THE LORD, THAT HE WILL INSTRUCT HIM? But we have the mind of Christ.

Now, let's apply this to Revelation 12, our focal passage for this study. Follow the whole chapter with me, and note the interplay between the *kairological* and the chronological:

- **Verses 1-2**

Now a great sign appeared in heaven: a woman clothed with the sun, with the moon under her feet, and on her head a garland of twelve stars. Then being with child, she cried out in labor and in pain to give birth.

John is seeing the "great sign in heaven" on the plane of kairological time, but the woman crying in in labor and pain during birth is chronological. Whatever is happening with her and her Child—and we know what it is—is a conjunction of kairos and kronos (which we would expect it to be since Jesus is the Messiah, fully divine and fully human).

- **Verses 3-5**

And another sign appeared in heaven: behold, a great, fiery red dragon having seven heads and ten horns, and seven diadems on his heads. His tail drew a third of the stars of heaven and threw them to the earth. And the dragon stood before the woman who was ready to give birth, to devour her Child as soon as it was born. She bore a male Child who was to rule all nations with a rod of iron. And her Child was caught up to God and His throne.

Now John is seeing the impact of the pre-creation fall of Lucifer, described in Isaiah 14, a kairological event, on situations in kronos-time. In fact, the fall of Lucifer occurs even before kronos is created. Then we see a compression in which a kronos-event, the birth of the male Child, is caught up into the kairos-level to God and His Throne. Again, this is an amazing clue and proof of Jesus as Messiah. If He is truly God and truly man, then kairos and kronos must intermingle in Him!

- **Verses 6-8**

Then the woman fled into the wilderness, where she has a place prepared by God, that they should feed her there one thousand two hundred and sixty days. And war broke out in heaven: Michael and his angels fought with the dragon; and the dragon and his angels fought, but they did not prevail, nor was a place found for them in heaven any longer.

The woman fleeing into the wilderness is a literal kronos event, the going of Israel and the seed of Israel into the Promised Land. The breaking out of war in heaven and the casting down of Lucifer and the fallen angels occurs on the kairos level, but will have effect on what happens to the woman and her Child on the kronos-plane.

- **Verses 9-10**

So the great dragon was cast out, that serpent of old, called the Devil and Satan, who deceives the whole world; he was cast to the earth, and his angels were cast out with him. Then I heard a loud voice saying in heaven, "Now salvation, and strength, and the kingdom of our God, and the power of His Christ have come, for the accuser of our brethren, who accused them before our God day and night, has been cast down.

Again, here is the intersection of kairos-time with kronos, but with a new element on the kronos-scale: Lucifer has been cast down before kronos, with the effect of his impact on all that exists on the kronos-level, but simultaneously the One Who enables us who live in kronos has also "come down." This is precisely what the Holy Spirit shows through Paul, in Ephesians 4:9-10--Notice that it says "he ascended." This means that Christ first came down to the lowly world in which we live. The same one who came down is the one who ascended higher than all the heavens, so that his rule might fill the entire universe. (NLT) Further, 2 Peter 3:10-12 reveals that Christ's rule of the whole universe will require a dramatic alteration in which kronos time is overwhelmed and displaced by kairos, the "dissolving" of the "elements of the universe" the Holy Spirit reveals in 2 Peter 3:10-12.

- **Verses 11-12**

And they overcame him by the blood of the Lamb and by the word of their testimony, and they did not love their lives to the death. Therefore rejoice, O heavens, and you who dwell in them! Woe to the inhabitants of the earth and the sea! For the devil has come down to you, having great wrath, because he knows that he has a short time."

The Greek translated "short time" refers to a brief moment within kronos when the devil's kairos intersects with and impacts events on the kronos plane. Sometimes I have stood on passenger rail platforms in Europe when an express train thunders through without stopping. For a brief moment the trajectory of the train, and all trailing with it— wind, dust, vibration, noise—impacts where I am standing. But it is quickly gone. So the devil's impact on our level of existence thunders through, but is quickly going.

- **Verses 13-14**

Now when the dragon saw that he had been cast to the earth, he persecuted the woman who gave birth to the male Child. But the woman was given two wings of a great eagle, that she might fly into the wilderness to her place, where she is nourished for a time and times and half a time, from the presence of the serpent.

Lucifer blinks his eyes and discovers he is now inhabiting the kronos level of existence. This is stunning to him because he realizes he is on the finite scale with all its limitations. With the aid of his principalities—his 'generals'—and their armies, he launches an assault on the 'woman,' now the summary figure of Israel. But she escapes into the special shelter God has made for her in the 'wilderness.' (More about this in the chapters ahead.)

- **Verses 15-17**

So the serpent spewed water out of his mouth like a flood after the woman, that he might cause her to be carried away by the flood. But the earth helped the woman, and the earth opened its mouth and swallowed up the flood which the dragon had spewed out of his mouth. And the dragon was enraged with the woman, and he went to make war with the rest of her offspring, who keep the commandments of God and have the testimony of Jesus Christ.   NKJV

Here we see a dazzling example of the interplay between the kairos-scale and the kronos-plane of time. Nature, the kronos-world, cooperates with kairological telos, the purposes of God beyond kronos-time, to fulfill the kairological purpose of God. The enemy having been defeated on the kairos-scale now focuses his attacks on the "offspring" of Israel, the authentic church existing on the kronos-level.

The fascinating truth is that Lucifer can no longer make war on the *kairos*-level, and his activity is now limited to the finite scale of *kronos* time.

I will leave you with this: All things are complete on the *kairological* level, meaning all reality at that scale is conformed to God's perfect intent. But that completeness is yet to be realized or manifest on the *kronos*-level. The events in the Middle East are therefore positive indicators because they are part of that grand movement toward completion of God's cosmic plan.

But because Jesus could say 'tetelestai' ('It is accomplished') on the cross—where kairos and kronos duel it out—the completion is also coming to the kronos-scale. And that's what the Second Coming of Jesus is all about!

WHILE GOD INHABITS THE *KAIROS* DIMENSION, HE IS CONSTANTLY STEPPING INTO THE *KRONOS* WORLD, IMPACTING THE LIVES OF THE "CONTRITE" AND "HUMBLE" AS THEY LIVE THEIR LIVES IN THE PROGRESSION OF PAST, PRESENT, AND FUTURE ALONG THE *KRONOS* TRACK.

Chapter 2

THE SPILLOVER EFFECT

One of the terrifying moments of my life occurred on a day in 1963. On my way to work after attending morning classes at Samford University in Birmingham, Alabama, I passed the high school from which I had graduated in 1960, and where my sister was still a student (she is seven years younger than I).

There are moments we call coincidence but which are really "Divine serendipities," surprise events that, as we reflect later, were acts of God's sovereign intervention. These are moments in our lives when *kairological* reality in the Kingdom of Heaven intersects with our *kronos* routines.

It was the day when our whites-only public high school was being desegregated and the exact moment when almost a thousand students ran outside and formed an angry mob.

I screeched to a halt, and tried to find my sister in the crowd. Soon I discovered she was one of only 12 students who had refused to protest the arrival of the school's first black students by going on strike. The mob began yelling her name, demanding that she come out and join them.

People were dying in Birmingham over civil rights in those days. I knew I had to rescue my sister. I ran into the school, and found her in a classroom. Somehow I was able to get her through the mob, and took her to the apartment where my wife and I lived in another part of our city, where my sister would be safe.

I have no idea how we got through that turbulent mob— it had to have been the Lord. All I can remember is trying to avoid what I would now call the "spillover effect": the flailing and growing violence that might hit us as innocent people trying to make our way in the middle of that situation.

The 'spillover effect'

On a far larger scale, that's what I mean in titling this book on Revelation 12, "Spillover." In this sense, "spillover" means that the effect of *kairological* realities is felt in our world, on the *kronos*-plane of time. The Revelation visions are all about the "spillover," or "fall-out" of the "War in Heaven" on our lives and institutions.

To grasp this, we have to go all the way back to Isaiah 14, which describes the fall of Lucifer. In Luke 10, Jesus is talking about His authority versus the power of Satan. Jesus says something strange as His disciples return from a successful mission for Christ's Kingdom: "I was watching Satan fall from heaven like lightning." (Luke 10:18) The Greek grammar here is interesting: Jesus was standing in His present *kronos* moment, watching a *kairos* event that had occurred before even the creation of the universe and *kronos*-

time. It is as if Jesus were saying, "While you were out on your mission I was watching Satan fall from heaven like lightning."

There are a couple of ways to understand this. First, maybe Jesus was watching the *kairological* event from the perspective of His pre-incarnate being. Or—and this is intriguing—perhaps the Kingdom missions of His people somehow are causes of the weakening of Satan, and the acceleration of his fall toward the lake of fire.

The implications of the biblical revelation of kairos-kronos time are stunning. As I taught on this topic a friend emailed me a question I thought was intriguing and provocative in a positive way. The writer alluded to the reference I made to Revelation 13:8, that Jesus is "the Lamb slain from the foundation of the world." So, my friend asked:

If the Lord God Almighty knew that Adam was going to sin, then did He decide that it was worth 70% of the human race in a devil's hell forever (assuming that's the percentage of all humans who have ever lived who have never heard the Gospel and had opportunity to respond to Christ)?

There are several replies I could give to that question, all based on Scripture, but I will answer in the context of our focus on the nature of time. *Theoretically, any omnipotent Being living in the kairos dimension could enter kronos at any point on its linear track.*

Think of the train on the track. The Omnipotent Being could go back to the *kronos* moment of the train's departure from the station of origination, or show up halfway on the journey, or appear on the train at its destination, still in the future. This is because *kairos* is tenseless in the sense of *kronos'* past, present, and future.

Here's the bombshell implication, which I will pose as a question: Is it possible that one of the dynamics of intercessory prayer is that it invites God to step back into the historical past in kronos-time, and redirect the course of the "train"? We in kronos-time would never know that was what happened, but would simply rest the matter with God in prayer. Who knows what situations God redirected in response to your prayers for the salvation of members of your family, or for their safety?

I pose my answers as questions because, as I wrote in the Introduction, we cannot make doctrine out of our speculations—including mine!—but only on the basis of biblical authority. And yet the implications of *kairos-kronos* might explain how humans can function with free will when it comes to accepting or rejecting Christ, and at the same time have their paths directed so they will at least have the opportunity.

God *is* the Omnipotent Being, and is transcendent, having His Being outside our dimension. Isaiah 15:57 especially reveals this reality about God:

For thus says the High and Lofty One Who inhabits eternity,
whose name is Holy:
"I dwell in the high and holy place,
With him who has a contrite and humble spirit,
To revive the spirit of the humble,
And to revive the heart of the contrite ones. (NKJV)

While God inhabits the *kairos* dimension, He is constantly stepping into the *kronos* world, impacting the lives of the "contrite" and "humble" as they live their lives in the progression of past, present, and future along the *kronos* track.

As I stressed above, the only way we can understand Revelation 12—and any part of the Bible's apocalyptic literature—is in the context of the nature of time. So, to comprehend the passage of our focus in this study, and set it in proper context, we must reach into other Revelation chapters:

- **Revelation 6:1-4**

Now I saw when the Lamb opened one of the seals; and I heard one of the four living creatures saying with a voice like thunder, "Come and see." And I looked, and behold, a white horse. He who sat on it had a bow; and a crown was given to him, and he went out conquering and to conquer. When He opened the second seal, I heard the second living creature saying, "Come and see." Another horse, fiery red, went out.

And it was granted to the one who sat on it to take peace from the earth, and that people should kill one another; and there was given to him a great sword.

What is revealed here is that when Christ and the Gospel enter the world in kronos-time, there is a counter-attack by the powers of darkness—war in heaven spilling over into the natural, finite world, as the next verses in Revelation 6 show:

- **Revelation 6:5-8**

When He opened the third seal, I heard the third living creature say, "Come and see." So I looked, and behold, a black horse, and he who sat on it had a pair of scales in his hand. And I heard a voice in the midst of the four living creatures saying, "A quart of wheat for a denarius, and three quarts of barley for a denarius; and do not harm the oil and the wine." When He opened the fourth seal, I heard the voice of the fourth living creature saying, "Come and see." So I looked, and behold, a pale horse. And the name of him who sat on it was Death, and Hades followed with him. And power was given to them over a fourth of the earth, to kill with sword, with hunger, with death, and by the beasts of the earth. NKJV

Revelation 11 prepares us for the things to be revealed in Revelation 12 by unveiling the future, and then linking it back to the past and present.

- **Revelation 11:15-12:4**

Then the seventh angel sounded; and there were loud voices in heaven, saying, " The kingdom of the world has become the kingdom of our Lord and of His Christ; and He will reign forever and ever." And the twenty-four elders, who sit on their thrones before God, fell on their faces and worshiped God, saying, "We give You thanks, O Lord God, the Almighty, who are and who were, because You have taken Your great power and have begun to reign. "And the nations were enraged, and Your wrath came, and the time came for the dead to be judged, and the time to reward Your bond-servants the prophets and the saints and those who fear Your name, the small and the great, and to destroy those who destroy the earth." And the temple of God which is in heaven was opened; and the ark of His covenant appeared in His temple, and there were flashes of lightning and sounds and peals of thunder and an earthquake and a great hailstorm.

This sets the stage for Revelation 12, and the War in Heaven, and its spillover effect into the kronos-world we presently inhabit (though there is a part of our being already "seated with Christ in heavenly places" [Ephesians 2:6], a tantalizing revelation we cannot explore in this study).

- **Revelation 12:1-2**

A great sign appeared in heaven: a woman clothed with the sun, and the moon under her feet, and on her head a crown of twelve stars; and she was with child; and she cried out, being in labor and in pain to give birth. Then another sign appeared in heaven: and behold, a great red dragon having seven heads and ten horns, and on his heads were seven diadems. And his tail swept away a third of the stars of heaven and threw them to the earth. And the dragon stood before the woman who was about to give birth, so that when she gave birth he might devour her child.

In an "unveiling" that sweeps across *kronos* time, placing it all on the stage of the *kairos*-perspective "on high," we see the actuality of the great strategic implementation of the fallen world's salvation.

We meet several women in Revelation—the "Jezebel" spirit of Revelation 2:20, the "harlot," who symbolizes the Babylonian world system opposed to God, and, on the positive side, the woman who is the "Bride" of Christ—the authentic Church. The woman of Revelation 12 falls also into that positive category: She represents Israel, the womb of the Messiah. This is not Mary, the chosen virgin only, though some of the things that happen to Mary and Joseph are types of that larger drama being played out with regard to Israel.

The first thing John sees in the Spirit—and reports to us—about this special woman is the way she appears in the eyes of the Omnipotent Being, the High and Holy One Who inhabits eternity.

First, she is "clothed with the sun." What does this mean in apocalyptic literature? Roman Catholics might say this is evidence of the glorious stature of Mary and compels veneration of her. But, as we will see, the context of Revelation 12 is not Mary, but Israel. To know what being "clothed with the sun" really means, we must go to the illumination and authority of Scripture, not human speculation.

"Clothed" is a Greek word signifying to be wrapped up in a garment. The woman of Revelation 12 is arrayed with the "sun" like an earthly queen draped in a dazzling robe. Again, Catholic theology for this reason refers to Mary as "the queen of heaven." But, again, Mary is not the subject of this vision, but Israel is. And since the authentic Church is the Bride of Christ, she is the "queen of Heaven."

Malachi 4:1-2, written more than 400 years before the Incarnation of God in Jesus Christ, gives illumination on the sun—excuse the pun:

> "For behold, the day is coming, burning like a furnace; and all the arrogant and every evildoer will be chaff; and the day that is coming will set them ablaze," says the LORD of hosts, "so that

it will leave them neither root nor branch. But for you who fear My name, the sun of righteousness will rise with healing in its wings; and you will go forth and skip about like calves from the stall."

This is a clear prophecy regarding the Messiah, Who, from Malachi's perspective, was yet to come. Jesus said of Himself, "I am the Light of the world; he who follows Me will not walk in the darkness, but will have the Light of life... While I am in the world, I am the Light of the world." (John 8:12; 9:5)

Notice an interesting implication: if the woman were presented as "clothing" the sun rather than the sun clothing the woman, then she would be cloaking the Light of the world. This is exactly what happens in dead religion, the religion of form but not power. (2 Timothy 3:5)

Therefore, it is Christ, the sun of righteousness, Who is to be seen in resplendent glory, not the human vessel. Since the woman is Israel, and since the Sun is Jesus the Christ, in all His radiant glory, then there is an obvious conclusion: the meaning and distinction of Israel is the Christ. Without Christ, Israel has no more resplendent garment than any other nation. But because she is predestined by God to be the vehicle by which the Sun of Righteousness will enter kronos-time, Israel is the truly exceptional nation in history. Note that this is Israel in its larger historical sense.

Second, the moon is under the woman's feet. There is much symbolism here. For one thing, the moon cannot generate its own light, but must reflect light. The true glory of people and nations is merely the radiation of the glory of the Sun of Righteousness. Also, the moon marks the seasons of earth within kronos time. But the woman, who we now see as spiritual Israel, encompassing the Church, is under the authority of the Sun of Righteousness (Matthew 28:18), and His authority spans all the seasons of creation and history.

The third thing revealed about the woman is that she is wearing a victory crown. There are two words in the Greek New Testament translated "crown." One is *diadema,* reserved exclusively for royalty—a king or queen. The other is *stephanos,* a victory garland given a competitor who wins a race or some match.

It is of much significance that the woman John sees in the vision is wearing a *stephanos,* not a *diadema.* The *diadema* is reserved for the Sun of Righteousness, the King of Kings alone. And the reason the woman can wear the *stephanos* even though she has not won the race or conquered the foe, is that she receives the glory and benefits of the One Who did win it all, the One Who wears the Diadem.

Think of the implications: You and I wear the victory crown because of Jesus, the King's victory! We did nothing to earn it ourselves. The *stephanos* is the crown of grace, and can only be given by the Victorious One Who wears the *Diadema.*

And here's another intriguing implication: Even though in kronos time at the point of the Birth of Christ, the victory is yet to be manifest, it is already manifest and accomplished in the kairos-realm. "It is finished!", still in kronos-future from the perspective of the Bethlehem manger, has already been shouted and declared in the kairos-realm!

That's why the woman, though in the labor that will bring forth the Messiah, is wearing the victory crown that marks the victory He will win in kronos-time. This brings the complete union of kairos and kronos reality, resulting in the salvation of the world. This all happens at the Cross!

Chapter 3

THE MYSTERY NATION

As if we didn't have enough to worry about, now comes word that the Carter-era NASA may have set us up for some real trouble—a literal spillover from the physical heavens.

Back in 1977 NASA launched Voyager 1. Its mission was

To explore strange new worlds

To seek out new life and new civilizations

To boldly go where no man has gone before

No, wait: That was the mission for the starship Enterprise, pronounced a decade earlier, in 1966. It only took the United States government 10 years to catch up with the Star Trek dream—lightspeed for federal bureaucracies.

Though the Enterprise exists only in a special effects studio and on Christmas trees throughout America, Voyager 1 was real, and, as we sit here, has now left our solar system. At the moment, Voyager 1 is 11.6 billion miles from earth, zipping into interstellar space, give or take a hundred million or so.

Voyager's primary mission is now completed, and now it is on to its secondary purpose—to find and introduce our planet and its species to ETs whose paths Voyager might cross.

A writer named Gerald D. Skoning says we need to worry.[2] Here's why, he says:

> Voyager carries "Golden Records" with warm greetings to any forms of extraterrestrial life it may encounter out there. It's a "welcome to Earth" message like a glossy advertising brochure for an exclusive vacation resort ("Come on down..."). Voyager's "Golden Record" contains beautiful, full color photos of the Earth, pictures of a man and woman, welcome messages and a promise that "we come in peace" from President Carter and then Secretary-General of the UN Boutros Boutros-Ghali, together with a chart of the solar system and detailed directions to our own jewel, planet Earth.

The romanticists of the Carter days assumed any ETs who got our invitation and detailed maps would be friendly, and if they weren't our kind greetings would pacify them.

---

[2] "Dangerous Alien Invitation?" By Gerald D. Skoning, *The American Spectator,* October 1, 2013. Retrieved from http://spectator.org/archives/2013/10/01/dangerous-alien-invitation.

We can't stop Voyager now, says Skoning, but, he writes, "on future missions into deep space, let's not invite "them" home for dinner, at least until we know who the heck they are!"

That brings up the tantalizing and chilling question: *What's out there?* Voyager hasn't found any ETs yet to report back, but the Bible shows us clearly: a "dragon" is out there, along with a horde of monsters, stirring chaos that spills over into our time-space zone!

In our last study we met the Woman of Revelation 12. The context of the rest of the chapter will show us that she is Israel. I said that this is Israel in the larger sense of God's cosmic plan of redemption, and not necessarily the geopolitical entity established in 1948.

Israel, past, present, and future

Let me expand a little on that. I do believe the geopolitical State of Israel will indeed play a significant role in events still future on the kronos-plane. However, that geopolitical Israel will be in a different form than it is now. We see this in Ezekiel 38. There, the Holy Spirit is revealing the assaults that will come on the geopolitical entity in that coming day from other geopolitical entities especially from the global north. The Lord instructs Ezekiel to say to Gog, the primary ruler of the anti-Israel coalition:

- **Ezek 38:10-12**

> 'Thus says the Lord GOD, "It will come about on that day, that thoughts will come into your mind and you will devise an evil plan, and you will say, 'I will go up against the land of unwalled villages. I will go against those who are at rest, that live securely, all of them living without walls and having no bars or gates, to capture spoil and to seize plunder, to turn your hand against the waste places which are now inhabited, and against the people who are gathered from the nations, who have acquired cattle and goods, who live at the center of the world.' NASU

Note this is a nation of "unwalled" villages. If you had traveled with Irene and me when we first went to Israel in 1981, we would have passed with some ease (except for a few military checkpoints) into Jericho and other West Bank villages and towns. Now, however, there is a massive wall that snakes along the West Bank boundaries. The Israel we know now is not "unwalled." However, there will come a time, says Revelation, when the threat against Israel will be diminished, and there will be no walls.

This will be a season in which Gog and the powers taking shape even now will see their opportunity to launch their all-out assault to carry out the mission they dream of now, and stated specifically by the Shiite rulers of Iran, to wipe Israel off the map. But it will actually be God Himself, in a Romans 1 tactic of removing His restraining hand, who lures them into their own destruction.

So the State of Israel established in 1948 is important, for two reasons:

1. The establishment of a shelter for Israel in the "wilderness," as Revelation 12 will point out.
2. A realm where *aliyah* can be implemented (the immigration of Jews from contemporary diaspora, as well as those who will immigrate in the future, fulfilling Jeremiah 16:14-15 (and other passages):

> the time is coming," says the LORD, "when people who are taking an oath will no longer say, 'As surely as the LORD lives, who rescued the people of Israel from the land of Egypt.' Instead, they will say, 'As surely as the LORD lives, who brought the people of Israel back to their own land from the land of the north and from all the countries to which he had exiled them.' For I will bring them back to this land that I gave their ancestors. NLT

Therefore the current State of Israel is important because it ultimately leads to the State that will exist in a time of "unwalled villages". Hardly anyone who thinks about the Middle East now has any hope for a solution. But the Bible shows that a time is coming when hostilities will have been reduced to such an extent that the massive wall that separates Israel from areas under control of the Palestinian authority will come down.

I am pro-Israel, but I am not anti-Palestinian. The most neglected and forgotten group of Christians on the earth today are the Palestinian followers of Jesus, wedged between Muslims who see them as turncoats and Jews who see them as nothing but a threat. Israel is an enigma for many. The very survival of the Jews is a mystery and a miracle. No people have ever had a greater degree of hatred or attempts at genocide against them than the Jews. Yet the tyrants who tried to purge earth of the Jews—from Nebuchadnezzar to Hitler, and many more—have themselves died away, but not the Jews.

The king of Prussia, Frederick the Great, in a discussion with his court chaplain once said, "Give me proof of the inspiration of the Bible."

The chaplain replied, "Your majesty, I can answer your request in a single word."

Frederick looked at the chaplain with some amazement and asked, "What magic word carries such strong proof?"

The chaplain answered, "Israel, your majesty."

Again and again the dragon has tried to eradicate the Jews from the earth. So, says Revelation 12:13-14, "when the dragon saw that he was thrown down to the earth, he persecuted the woman who gave birth to the male child."

Why? Because Israel is the womb through which the "Male Child"—the Messiah—would enter the created world. Why the passion to persecute the woman? Because Israel is the world's pivotal nation. Prior to Israel the nations saw time as completely cyclical—an endless, hopeless rotation of birth, death, rebirth-reincarnation forever. But through God's revelation entrusted to the Hebrew heart, history was revealed as also linear, meaning its circling events were not static, but moving forward toward goal and purpose—the coming of Messiah and the new heavens and the new earth foreseen by Hebrew prophets.

Paul Johnson, one of the greatest contemporary historians, put it this way: "No people has ever insisted more firmly than the Jews that history has a purpose and humanity a destiny... The Jews, therefore, stand right at the centre of the perennial attempt to give human life the dignity of a purpose."[3]

---

[3]Paul Johnson, *A History of the Jews* (HarperCollins, New York, ©1987, p. 2)

Michael Novak is one of my favorite Catholic writers in his critiques of culture. In one of his books he points out the pivotal role of Israel for the formation of the United States:

> "The Bible was the one book that literate Americans in the seventeenth, eighteenth, and nineteenth centuries could be expected to know well," Robert Bellah has written. "Biblical imagery provided the basic framework for imaginative thought in America up until quite recent times and, unconsciously, its control is still formidable." As a design for the Seal of the United States, Jefferson suggested "a representation of the children of Israel in the wilderness, led by a cloud by day and a pillar of fire by night." He later concluded his second inaugural address with this same image: "I shall need ... the favor of that Being in whose hands we are, who led our fathers, as Israel of old, from their native land and planted them in a country flowing with all the necessaries and comforts of life."
>
> The image of "God's American Israel" ... brought to intense focus by the Americans in a new and historically original way. The first of these new perspectives was a narrative of purpose and progress. The Gentiles of the ancient world

believed in cycles of time as regular (they thought) as the circular movements of the stars. They believed in eternal recurrence. But the Americans of 1770-1799 did *not* believe that time is cyclical, going nowhere, spinning in circles pointlessly. They believed that history had a *beginning* and was guided by Providence for a *purpose*... Time (in the view of the founders) was created for the *unfolding of human liberty*, for human emancipation. This purpose requires humans to choose for or against building cities worthy of the ideals God sets before them: liberty, justice, equality, self-government, and brotherhood...

Nowadays, even secular people interpret history in the light of progress, rights, and liberty. Yet unbelievers received these concepts neither from the Greeks and Romans nor from Enlightened Reason, but via the preaching of Jesus Christ, from whom the Gentiles learned the essential outlook of the Hebrews: that the Creator gave humans a special place among all other creatures, and made them free, and endowed them with incomparable responsibility and dignity.

This sequence of related conceptions - that time had a *beginning* and is *measured for progress (or decline)* by God's standards; that everything in the world is intelligible, and that to *inquire, invent,* and *discover is an impulse of faith* as well as of reason; that the *Creator endowed us with liberty and inviolable dignity,* while the Divine Judge shows concern for *the weak and the humble*; that life is a *time of duty and trial*; and that history is to be grasped as *the drama of human liberty* - all these are the background that make sense of the Declaration of Independence. America and Israel, the first Israel and the second, shed light on each other...[4]

'Devouring' the Baby

As we have seen, there is a "cosmic" Israel and a historic, biological Israel. By "cosmic" I mean there is a body of people, a nation, through whom God will work His sovereign purposes. Historical Israel is the manifestation in time and

[4] *On Two Wings: Humble Faith and Common Sense at the American Founding*, by Michael Novak (Encounter Books, San Francisco, CA, ©2002, pp. 8-12.

space of that cosmic reality in the mind and plan of God. Cosmic Israel is in view in Revelation 12 where the war in the heavens is fought, and there is spillover—a whole torrent—on historic Israel.

A primary reason we know cosmic Israel is in view in Revelation 12 is the strategy of the Dragon toward the Woman and her Baby, revealed in the passages we look at in this study.

Israel is the womb of the Messiah, and the Dragon wants to catch and destroy the Baby as it comes from the womb. Here's what the Scripture says, in Revelation 12:3-4:

> Then another sign appeared in heaven: and behold, a great red dragon having seven heads and ten horns, and on his heads were seven diadems. And his tail swept away a third of the stars of heaven and threw them to the earth. And the dragon stood before the woman who was about to give birth, so that when she gave birth he might devour her child.

As we noted in preceding chapters, this is a sweeping compression of kairos-time into a kronos-historical event. We have the pre-creation, pre-kronos fall of Lucifer, and we see the "spillover" into a specific historical event, the Birth of Jesus of Nazareth.

Herod's slaughter of the Bethlehem babies was a spillover into kronos of the kairos-vision of the dragon trying to destroy the Baby. In a sense, Herod was acting as the "earth-beast" in this case, driven by the antichrist spirit, to try to destroy the Baby almost from the womb. Herod learns from the Wise Men about the Birth of the Messiah in Bethlehem, and he orders the execution of all Bethlehem's babies two and under, in an attempt to "gobble" up the Child born of Israel's womb, in and through the Virgin Mary.

The spirit driving the abortion worldview of our time is a spillover of this passion to destroy the Ultimate Infant. In case society forgets the monstrous nature of abortion, every now and then arises a Kermit Gosnell and his hideous crimes committed in the dark corners of his abortion clinic, as well as the pro-abortion protestors who proclaimed their worship of Satan and hatred of the church as they chanted their mantras during the 2013 Texas Legislature debate on imposing restrictions on abortion clinics.

The dazzling dragon: A universal 'archetype'

Who is this 'Dragon,' and why is the imagery of a dragon used to describe him? The Greek word is *drakown* (δρακων). This term is used 12 times in the Book of Revelation to refer to the Devil. The word carries the idea of a winged serpent with a striking, dazzling appearance.

This symbol is found in almost all cultures across the world, throughout history. Carl Jung, a Swiss psychoanalyst, developed the theory of "archetypes," which are "universal, archaic patterns and images that derive from the collective unconscious." While there is much with which we would disagree in Jung's thought, he seems to be right about the archetype phenomena, and the dragon imagery of Revelation would provide evidence. It is part of the "collective unconscious," meaning the image is present in some form in all human beings. J.E. Cirlot, an expert on cultural and religious symbols, says the dragon symbol "is a kind of amalgam (amalgamation, fusion, mix) of elements taken from various animals that are particularly aggressive and dangerous..."[5]

The Greek, *drakown,* is from a root meaning, "to see," as in looking on something amazing and astonishing that makes you want to keep looking. It might also signify the fiery, piercing eyes of a creature that sears right into the depths of your being.

One scholar says the dragon imagery embedded in the human consciousness may have derived from the remains of "antediluvian (pre-Flood) monsters."[6] Perhaps, even, the dragon archetype was embedded in the human psyche from

---

[5] J.E. Cirlot, *A Dictionary of Symbols,* New York, Barnes & Noble, 1995, pages 85ff.
[6] *Ibid.*

the Garden of Eden itself. The ancient Gnostics saw the dragon as the symbol of chaos, which is certainly what the serpent introduced into Eden.

The Bible gives us a rich flow of information, especially about the astonishing appearance of the "dragon":

- **Isaiah 14:12**

  "How you have fallen from heaven,

  O star of the morning, son of the dawn!

- **Ezekiel 28:12-15**

  "You had the seal of perfection,

  Full of wisdom and perfect in beauty.

  "You were in Eden, the garden of God;

  Every precious stone was your covering:

  The ruby, the topaz and the diamond;

  The beryl, the onyx and the jasper;

  The lapis lazuli, the turquoise and the emerald;

  And the gold, the workmanship of your settings and sockets,

  Was in you.

  On the day that you were created

  They were prepared.

  "You were the anointed cherub who covers,

  And I placed you there.

  You were on the holy mountain of God;

  You walked in the midst of the stones of fire.

  "You were blameless in your ways

From the day you were created

Until unrighteousness was found in you.

- **Genesis 3:1**

Now the serpent was more crafty than any beast of the field which the LORD God had made. And he said to the woman, "Indeed, has God said, 'You shall not eat from any tree of the garden'?

But 700 years before Christ's coming, Isaiah sees the ultimate defeat of the dragon. God allows Isaiah to see at the kairological plane what is even now in the kronos-future for us: In that day the LORD will punish Leviathan the fleeing serpent, With His fierce and great and mighty sword, Even Leviathan the twisted serpent; And He will kill the dragon who lives in the sea. (Isaiah 27:1)

The power of the Dragon

What the Bible is telling us is that in the kairos-realm there is a being who is the adversary of the Kingdom of Heaven, and who has an army of the demonic waging war that spills over and impacts the kronos realm.

Notice again what John sees about the dragon in his vision:

- **Rev 12:3**

Then another sign appeared in heaven: and behold, a great red dragon *having seven heads and ten horns, and on his heads were seven diadems*. NASU

To understand this we need to reach back to the apocalyptic visions of Daniel.

- **Dan 7:15-18**

"As for me, Daniel, my spirit was distressed within me, and the visions in my mind kept alarming me. I approached one of those who were standing by and began asking him the exact meaning of all this. So he told me and made known to me the interpretation of these things: 'These great beasts, which are four in number, are four kings who will arise from the earth. But the saints of the Highest One will receive the kingdom and possess the kingdom forever, for all ages to come.' NASU

What Daniel has seen that distresses him so much is the rise of four world empires that will surface again and again in history—kairological realities circling along the line of kronos. These will be kingdoms, or dominions, under the control of the Dragon, the meaning of the heads, horns, and diadems. These reoccurring realms comprise the Babylonian world system revealed as the attempt to order the world without God and in defiance of God.

Every civilization across history, including those of the present, is simply a manifestation of one or more of those types of empire. These empires are ruled by mighty principalities, who are the generals of the Dragon. Their great mission is to fight against the rule of God's Son on earth. (This is the imagery we see in the White Horse and Red Horse.)

Daniel sees important detail about these four types of empire. This detail is revealed as the Holy Spirit enables Daniel to interpret a dream experienced by King Nebuchadnezzar:

- **Dan 2:36-40**

> "This is the dream. Now we will tell the interpretation of it before the king. You, O king, are a king of kings. For the God of heaven has given you a kingdom, power, strength, and glory; and wherever the children of men dwell, or the beasts of the field and the birds of the heaven, He has given them into your hand, and has made you ruler over them all — you are this head of gold. But after you shall arise another kingdom inferior to yours; then another, a third kingdom of bronze, which shall rule over all the earth. And the fourth kingdom shall be as strong as iron, inasmuch as iron breaks in pieces and

shatters everything; and like iron that crushes, that kingdom will break in pieces and crush all the others. NKJV

The Babylonian Composite

Because the Holy Spirit reveals the historic chronological procession of these kingdoms, we know exactly what they are, and the characteristic they bring to the nations of the world system that will resist Christ and His Kingdom rule:

- *Babylon*—the Empire of human 'messiahs'
- *Persia*—The Empire of militarism (we should not be surprised at current events related to Iran)
- *Greece*—the Empire of cultural dominance (this is the battle for biblical values in western culture now being waged)
- *Rome*—The Empire of elitist dominance (now the elites of Entertainment, Information, Academia, and Politics)

These empires are all under the control of the Antichrist, the primary agent within humanity of the dragon's agenda. I call this "The Babylon Composite" because there is an element of each of these in the Babylonian world system revealed in the Revelation visions given to John.

Remember, the dragon is trying to devour the Baby. Herod's massacre was a literal, kronos-level manifestation of that. However, the Dragon will try to consume every advance of Christ's Kingdom, and that's why we are constantly engaged in spiritual warfare.

Evil and Love

Why would God allow the rebellion of Lucifer? Why would God allow evil to spill over into the world of space, kronos-time, and matter? This leads us to the doctrine of theodicy, the doctrine of evil.

Remember, God is love. He creates us in His image, meaning we have the capacity to love. But love requires freedom—for no one can be forced to love—freedom mandates choice, and choice necessitates options, like between good and evil; therefore, evil must be permitted, even though the cost will be highest for God above all, which we see in the Cross, and in the words of Jesus, in John 15:13: "Greater love has no one than this, that one lay down his life for his friends."

Therefore, Revelation 12, which focuses on God's cosmic plan for the reconciliation of all things to Himself is about "War in Heaven," but it is also about love.

THE GREATEST MISTAKE MANY MAKE IN

INTERPRETING REVELATION IS NOT KNOWING OR

FORGETTING WHAT THE BIBLE REVEALS ABOUT

THE NATURE OF TIME. THE BIBLICAL VIEW OF

TIME STRAIGHTENS OUT MUCH CONFUSION IN THE

INTERPRETATION OF THE BOOK OF

REVELATION—AS WELL AS ALL PROPHETIC AND

APOCALYPTIC LITERATURE IN THE BIBLE.

Chapter 4

THE BIG STORY

I am an avid news reader. I prefer taking in detail, and having time to reflect on it. So much broadcast journalism is a Big Mac on the run. I like to savor and think.

Sound-bite news helps explain what has gone so terribly wrong in culture. I call it Barney Fife journalism. Barney (Don Knotts) was the hapless deputy under Sheriff Andy Taylor (Andy Griffith) in Mayberry. Barney the bungler is destined to get things wrong.

One day he happens by a jewelry store where Andy and his lady-friend have just bought a bracelet she is to give someone. While the jeweler goes to the back of the shop, Andy and Helen steal a kiss. Barney, outside, sees the couple kiss, and assumes they have just bought a wedding ring.

Barney now has a scoop that he spreads all over Mayberry. He and Thelma Lou, his girlfriend, along with Aunt Bee, who lives with Andy and his son Opie, plan a surprise engagement party. They even remodel Andy's bedroom to make it less male-oriented, and more appropriate for a husband and wife.

This is a parable of the nature of news dissemination in our day. Reporters see an event, draw their conclusions about it, and squeeze it into a 30-second or one minute at most sound-bite. Viewers and listeners make plans around the information, and even redesign their worldview and worlds to accommodate the dazzling new reportage.

They even elect politicians who have become master of the sound-bite rather than people with substantive experience and knowledge.

Sadly, most of the time, this kind of news reporting, like Barney Fife, either gets it terribly wrong, or leaves out the important information that would give a more complete understanding.

Sometimes sound-bite newscasters miss the atom bomb of the big story while making the BB of the trivial sound like a nuclear blast.

That's exactly what's happening in our culture. Hundreds of millions of people are missing the Big Story. The sound-bites are enough. This is sad, because "current events" is too narrowly focused on the *kronos*-plane.

The Big Story is *kairos*-reality intersecting the *kronos*-time line, using it as a track to convey the actuality of the Kingdom of Heaven—the Third Heaven—into the First Heaven, the dimension of time and space that we inhabit in our bodies.

THIRD HEAVEN

INFINITY: KAIROS	KAIROS	KAIROS
KAIROS	KAIROS	KAIROS
KAIROS	KAIROS	

SECOND HEAVEN   **FIRST HEAVEN**

UNIVERSE: KRONOS   KRONOS
KRONOS

KRONOS   KRONOS   KRONOS

KAIROS   KAIROS   KAIROS   KAIROS

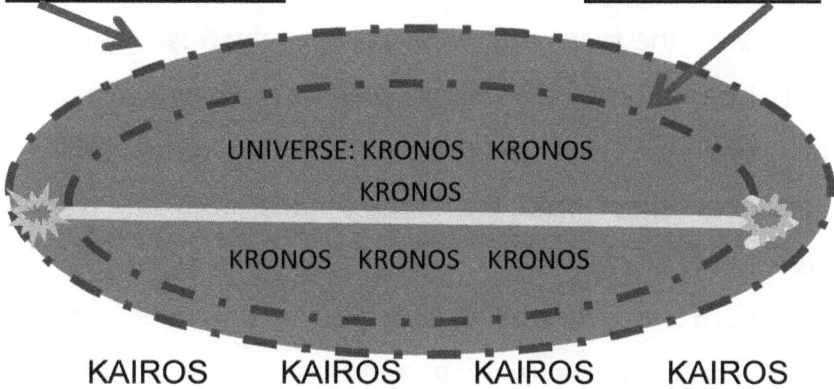

We see such an interaction between *kairos* actuality and *kronos* reality in Revelation 12. As we focus in on Revelation 12:5-6, we gain some special insights into this amazing interaction that give us important information but also hope and encouragement. This does not emerge in a mere "sound-bite" study, and this is why I am lingering over these passages. I want you to come to the place of hope and encouragement.

Revelation 12:5-6 is our focus in this chapter:

> And she gave birth to a son, a male child, who is to rule all the nations with a rod of iron; and her child was caught up to God and to His

throne. Then the woman fled into the wilderness where she had a place prepared by God, so that there she would be nourished for one thousand two hundred and sixty days. NASU

Here's the focus that emerges from the text: There is a specified period in God's cosmic plan that spans kairos and kronos, when the Covenant People of God are protected from the spillover effect onto the kronos-plane from the war in heaven.

There's an overarching principle that emerges from this fact: *God will always have a remnant people, a remnant community that He preserves through every cataclysm to represent the interests and cause of the Kingdom of God.*

Biblical Numerology

Since salvation history and the challenges to the remnant community appear across kronos-time, and since kronos-time is the quantitative measure of events and their processes, numbers are important in the Bible. However, as I discussed in the Introduction to this book, we must not allow numerology to lure us into speculative interpretation and theology.

Again, *we must allow the Bible to say what it says.*

What "counts" with biblical numerology is the fact that the events described throughout Scripture are actual. They are not mythological as Thomas Jefferson and other rationalist Deists of the 19th century and other eras have taught. The miracles, the tribulations and trials, the victories—culminating in Christ's atonement and resurrection—are historic events, quantifiable on human calendars. This is why the Bible spends so much focus on the reigns of potentates, from the Old Testament kings to the Roman rulers of the New Testament era. It's as if the Bible were telling us, "this (or that) event happened during the Bush Administration... the Obama Administration," etc.

Second, measurable numbers in the Bible express duration. This means events are finite, having their boundaries of beginning and end. For example, in the message to the Smyrna Church appearing in Revelation 2:9-10, Jesus says,

> 'I know your tribulation and your poverty (but you are rich), and the blasphemy by those who say they are Jews and are not, but are a synagogue of Satan. 'Do not fear what you are about to suffer. Behold, the devil is about to cast some of you into prison, so that you will be tested, and *you will have tribulation for ten days*. Be faithful until death, and I will give you the crown of life. (NASB, italics added)

The Lord is assuring His people suffering in Smyrna that their pain is of limited duration, and then will come victory, "the crown of life."

The same principle applies with the 1,000-year rule of Christ and His remnant community mentioned in Revelation 20. There will be a period in kronos-history when blessing will characterize the nations as they come into consensus about Jesus Christ and the importance of following Him. The specification of number lets us know this is not fantasy, but will be historical fact.

The numerics, like the 144,000 end-time witnesses of Revelation 7 and 14, 1,260 days of Revelation 12 and other numbered groups and times reveal what will happen as tangible realities in the pivotal intersections of kairos and kronos.

As we saw earlier, these intersections are marked in the Bible as the "fullness of time". For example, Galatians 4:4-5 tells us that "when the fullness of the time came, God sent forth His Son, born of a woman, born under the Law, so that He might redeem those who were under the Law, that we might receive the adoption as sons."

"Fullness", in New Testament Greek, is *pleroma,* referring to that which makes something complete, or full. Kronos-time exists as the vehicle in the time-space-matter world that will provide the junction-points for kairological interaction. Think of electrical wiring. A copper strand has one purpose, and that is to provide points of linkage with a power source. When the connection is made, the "fullness" or completeness of the copper wire has been met.

Sometimes the number designations in the Bible are clearly presented as literal, as in the measure of days between the Day of Atonement and Pentecost, or the period of time between Jesus' death on the cross and His resurrection. At other points we are not certain whether the number designations are literal or not because the Bible doesn't say so specifically. But this we can always know: *Biblical numberings always specify the absolute certainty that the connection between kairos and kronos will occur, and that the reality of the Kingdom of Heaven will be manifest in the world.*

Jesus Christ is the Intersection Point for all kronos-time. This is why His birth marks the "fullness" of kronos-time. Galatians 4:4 says that when that moment was reached, "God sent forth His Son, born of a woman..." The concept of "sending" infers being dispatched from one location to another on special mission. Jesus was co-existent with the Father (John 17) in the Third Heaven—the highest—where kairos is the time-expression, and in His incarnation He joins Himself to the kronos-dimension. So the Christ came from the kairos-actuality into the kronos-context. This will happen again in the Second Coming.

At this point, it will help to return to a previous metaphor, that of kronos-time as a railroad track. The laying of the "track" of time began with the laying of the "foundation" of the material world. (Revelation 13:8 KJV) There is a build-up along the track of typological and prophetic witness whereby the Messiah will be recognized and confirmed when He appears "down the track". Past, present, and future—tenses of kronos—are essential for this acceleration toward the *pleroma* of kronos-time.

However, the singularity of Jesus Christ is that He will inhabit kronos while retaining His Being in the kairos-realm. To do this He must have human biology that enables Him to live in the material world. This will be possible only if He enters the kronos-world through a human womb requiring kronos-numbered gestation. Yet Jesus the Christ will be sinless, an essential qualification for His atonement mission. Therefore He cannot have the sin-guilt passed down the line of Adam. The virgin birth is thus another essential that qualifies Jesus for His mission of being Savior of the world.

Philippians 2:5-11 reveals this:

> Let this mind be in you which was also in Christ Jesus, who, being in the form of God, did not consider it robbery to be equal with God, but made Himself of no reputation, taking the form of a bondservant, and coming in the likeness of men. And being found in appearance as a man, He humbled Himself and became obedient to the point of death, even the death of the cross.

Therefore God also has highly exalted Him and given Him the name which is above every name, that at the name of Jesus every knee should bow, of those in heaven, and of those on earth, and of those under the earth, and that every tongue should confess that Jesus Christ is Lord, to the glory of God the Father. (NKJV)

Therefore, again, *the intersection (or junction) between kairos and kronos is in Jesus Christ.* Jesus of Nazareth, the Christ, is the first human being to inhabit both the kairos and kronos dimensions simultaneously!

The Transfiguration shows this graphically. Matthew's Gospel describes what happened:

Six days later Jesus took with Him Peter and James and John his brother, and led them up on a high mountain by themselves. And He was transfigured before them; and His face shone like the sun, and His garments became as white as light. And behold, Moses and Elijah appeared to them, talking with Him. Peter said to Jesus, "Lord, it is good for us to be here; if You wish, I will make three tabernacles here, one for You, and one for Moses, and one for Elijah." While he was still speaking, a bright cloud overshadowed them, and behold, a voice out of the cloud said, "This is My beloved Son, with whom I am well-pleased; listen to Him!" When the disciples heard this, they fell face down to the ground and were terrified. And Jesus came to them and touched them and said, "Get up, and do not be afraid." And lifting up their eyes, they saw no one except Jesus Himself alone.

"Six days later" is a vital element in the stunning event on the mount. The phrase stipulates that the Transfiguration occurs through the interaction of kairos and kronos, and that it is manifest on the human clock and calendar though it is a kairological event.

That brings us back to the principle presented at the beginning of this chapter: What "counts" with biblical numerology is the fact that the events described throughout Scripture are actual in kronos-time, and are compressed within its limits even though they are the realities that have being on the kairos-level.

Chapter 5

THE THREE HEAVENS

Ecclesiastes 3:11 says God has put "eternity" in the human heart. That is, the human being, God's image-bearer, is conscious there is a realm beyond space and time, and has the capacity to reflect on it, and, through Christ, even commune and interact with it.

It should not surprise us, then, that the structure of human nations tends to be like the structure of the Three Heavens that presently comprise the composite of all reality.

For example, we speak of the federal government, state government, and local (municipal) government. These have varying degrees of authority and power in different nations.

This is the backdrop for Revelation 12:7-12, on which we've aimed our focus in these studies.

> And there was war in heaven, Michael and his angels waging war with the dragon. The dragon and his angels waged war, and they were not strong enough, and there was no longer a place found for them in heaven. And the great dragon was thrown down, the serpent of old who is

called the devil and Satan, who deceives the whole world ; he was thrown down to the earth, and his angels were thrown down with him. Then I heard a loud voice in heaven, saying, "Now the salvation, and the power, and the kingdom of our God and the authority of His Christ have come, for the accuser of our brethren has been thrown down, he who accuses them before our God day and night. And they overcame him because of the blood of the Lamb and because of the word of their testimony, and they did not love their life even when faced with death. For this reason, rejoice, O heavens and you who dwell in them. Woe to the earth and the sea, because the devil has come down to you, having great wrath, knowing that he has only a short time."

The only way to understand internal conflict within a nation is in the context of the varying levels of authority and power. The same is true in understanding the cosmic battle. We must consider—as we have above—the nature of time, and also the nature of the Three Heavens, the three "jurisdictions" of all cosmic order.

The fundamental principle of biblical hermeneutics (the science of interpretation) is that *Scripture interprets Scripture.*

This means we may consult commentaries and historical understandings, but always the ultimate standard of scriptural interpretation is the Bible itself, and its full context.

Therefore, to understand the idea of "war in heaven" we must set the topic into the context of the whole of Scripture. As we have seen, the Bible's revelation of the nature of time is vital for all biblical interpretation, and especially for the apocalyptic and prophetic.

By the way, the fact of the Bible's revelation of the nature of time leads to an interesting view of science. We speak of science "discovering" facts and truths about whatever it is investigating. "Discovery" infers that the something so discovered has always been there. The early "discoverers" of the Americas simply found what already existed.

Therefore, the Bible's revelation of time is absolute, and truths contemporary science discovers are discoverable because they are already there. A major feature of the Christian Theistic Worldview is that the world is intelligible. But this is only because of the principle of correspondence: God has created His image-bearers with a mind that can correspond to the reality to be discovered. Some worldviews hold that the world is meaningless and not understandable. But the fact of our being made in the Image of God means we are uniquely gifted to discover and understand what He has made. In this sense, science is therefore like a key and keyhole: the human brain is capable of understanding what is already there.

Crucial distinction

So here's the crucial distinction: *Science discovers the reality the Bible already knows because its Author is the One Who brought all reality into existence.*

We have learned that kairos is time-in-continuum, while kronos is time-in-process. There are important events in the Bible that show this.

First, the Transfiguration of Jesus. In that extraordinary kronos moment, there is confluence with the Third Heaven and its time-continuum. I use "confluence" rather than "convergence" or "merger" for a specific reason. "Confluence" means a flowing together of two streams at a specific point or juncture.[7] That confluence is not necessarily unending because there may come a fork where the streams diverge again.

As we will see there are many confluences of kairos-kronos in the Bible. However, the existence of two levels of time—that of the Third Heaven and that of the First Heaven—will end when kairos and kronos collide at the Day of the Lord. Out of that conflagration will come, not confluence, not even convergence, but *fusion,* a qualitatively *kainos*-new (to finite

---

[7] http://www.thefreedictionary.com/confluence.

reality) quality of time—one that is a continuum, like kairos, but is also experience of various phenomena in a sequential pattern that inhabitants can enter at any point—"past, present, future."

This is what happens through that event Peter describes in 2 Peter 3:10-13:

> But the day of the Lord will come like a thief, and then the heavens will vanish (pass away) with a thunderous crash, and the [material] elements [of the universe] will be dissolved with fire, and the earth and the works that are upon it will be burned up. Since all these things are thus in the process of being dissolved, what kind of person ought [each of] you to be [in the meanwhile] in consecrated *and* holy behavior and devout *and* godly qualities, While you wait and earnestly long for (expect and hasten) the coming of the day of God by reason of which the flaming heavens will be dissolved, and the [material] elements [of the universe] will flare *and* melt with fire? But we look for new heavens and a new earth according to His promise, in which righteousness (uprightness, freedom from sin, and right standing with God) is to abide. (Amplified Bible)

Note especially the term "abide". That refers to the Continuum, which is a quality of kairos. Right now the righteousness of God does not always "abide" in the world. There is a falling away, apostasy throughout history. Apostasy will be widespread in the Last Days. But in the New Heavens and New Earth, there is existence in what seems to be kronos, but infused with kairos-continuity, meaning, among other things, the continuum of holiness and purity in the whole world.

Confluence, not convergence

So, at the Mount of Transfiguration, we see confluence, not convergence, and certainly not fusion. Moses and Elijah, living fully in the eternal continuum of kairos, appear with Jesus, the God-Man, fully human, fully divine, and therefore existing in both kairos and kronos. Moses and Elijah cannot step into kronos but the Son of God can enter kairos fully to converse with them.

The key leadership core of disciples, Peter, James, and John, is allowed to see this to confirm that the Person in Whom they have placed their faith and commitment is exactly Who He says He is. "Transfigure" means to strip away an outer shell or covering so that we can see the true nature, the actual reality. Thus, in this confluence of kairos and kronos, Peter, James, and John see Jesus as He really is.

But because the Great Fusion of 2 Peter 3 has not yet come, kronos takes over. Peter doesn't want to leave the place of confluence, but the Father Himself tells Peter to focus on Jesus and listen to Him, not his own soulish desires.

In the Revelation visions John finds himself caught up by the Spirit so that he sees kairological reality about history. In Revelation 4:1-2 John tells us

> After these things I looked, and behold, a door *standing* open in heaven, and the first voice which I had heard, like *the sound* of a trumpet speaking with me, said, "Come up here, and I will show you what must take place after these things." Immediately I was in the Spirit; and behold, a throne was standing in heaven, and One sitting on the throne. (Emphasis added)

A door denotes a passage. A passage signifies a corridor through a barrier that would prevent access if the passage and door were not there. Thus there is an obstructing object between where John is on the Isle of Patmos which is on the earth, which is in the First Heaven, and the reality in the Third Heaven. This obstruction is the Second Heaven.

This is apparently what Ezekiel sees in his vision of the heavenlies, given in Ezekiel 1.

Now it came about in the thirtieth year, on the fifth day of the fourth month, while I was by the river Chebar among the exiles, the heavens were opened and I saw visions of God... Now *over the heads* of the living beings there was something like an expanse, like the awesome gleam of crystal, spread out over their heads... And there came a voice *from above the expanse* that was over their heads; whenever they stood still, they dropped their wings. Now *above the expanse* that was over their heads there was something resembling a throne... (Verses 1, 22, 25-26)

This may be the significance of the "veil" in the Temple, establishing a barrier between the areas accessible to humans and the Holy of Holies. Perhaps this obstruction is the meaning of Hebrews 6:19-20: "This hope we have as an anchor of the soul, a hope both sure and steadfast and one which enters within the veil, where Jesus has entered as a forerunner for us, having become a high priest forever according to the order of Melchizedek..."

In a moment we will see just how much of an obstruction the Second Heaven is, and what it takes to penetrate it.

Before we look more closely at this let's review a couple of important things. In 2 Corinthians 12:3 Paul refers expressly to the Third Heaven, and identifies it as the Throne of God (which is why the Old Testament often refers to God as the "Most High"). If there is a Third Heaven, there has to be a First and Second Heaven. What are they?

"Heaven" is *ouranos* in New Testament Greek. The word has several meanings: the expanse of the sky and all visible in it, as well as space. But the most intriguing here is that *ouranos,* according to the *Thayer and Smith Greek Lexicon,* also means "the seat of order of things eternal and consummately perfect where God dwells..."

Each *ouranos,* then, has thrones, but only by intent or permission of the Occupant of the Throne of the Third Heaven, Who is over all. God's image-bearers are given the throne in the First Heaven by the direct intention of God. Satan occupies the throne of the Second Heaven, only by the permission of God in allowing Satan's rebellion.

Now, we can better understand the "war in heaven". It is the war between the authorities of the Third Heaven and the powers of the Second Heaven for the destiny of the First Heaven. And, this raging conflict between the "hosts" of the Third Heaven and the fallen angels of the Second Heaven has spillover into the First Heaven.

There are important implications here for us.

The Second Heaven is an imposition, with Lucifer, the Dragon, seizing power from the Most High rather than it being granted to him. And this also explains why Lucifer, the beautiful angel who became a beast is so intent on making war with the Covenant Community, the "offspring of the woman" (Israel).

The covenant Community is that remnant that continues to walk in the covenant of blood struck in history with Abraham, and fulfilled in the descendant of Abraham's line, Jesus of Nazareth, the Christ.

The first Adam turned over his dominion in the First Heaven to Lucifer when he appeared in the Garden and seduced Adam and Eve. Here are some Scriptures that report the outcome of that tragic decision:

- **John 12:27-32**

  "Now My soul has become troubled; and what shall I say, ' Father, save Me from this hour'? But for this purpose I came to this hour. Father, glorify Your name." Then a voice came out of heaven: "I have both glorified it, and will glorify it again." So the crowd of people who stood by and heard it were saying that it had thundered; others were saying, " An angel has spoken to Him." Jesus answered and said, " This voice has not come for My sake, but for your sakes. Now judgment is upon this world; now *the ruler of this world* will be cast out. 32 "And I, if I am lifted up from the earth, will draw all men to Myself. (Emphasis added)

- **John 14:30**

  "I will not speak much more with you, for *the ruler of the world* is coming, and he has nothing in Me..." (Emphasis added)

- **John 16:8-11**

  "And He (the Holy Spirit), when He comes, will convict the world concerning sin and righteousness and judgment; concerning sin, because they do not believe in Me; and concerning righteousness, because I go to the Father and you no longer see Me; and concerning judgment, because *the ruler of this world* has been judged." (Emphasis added)

- **1 John 5:18-19**

  We know that no one who is born of God sins; but He who was born of God keeps him, and the evil one does not touch him. We know that we are of God, and that *the whole world lies in the power of the evil one.* (Emphasis added)

But the Second Adam, Jesus Christ, brought the rule of the Kingdom with Him, and gave it to all who would be restored to the Covenant through His Blood. Therefore it is the Covenant Community that now holds dominion in the created realm. Therefore, Revelation 1:5- tells us, "To Him who loves us and released us from our sins by His blood — and He has made us to be a kingdom, priests to His God and Father — to Him be the glory and the dominion forever and ever. Amen."

Other passages show this same reality.

- **Revelation 5:6-10**

    And I saw between the throne (with the four living creatures) and the elders a Lamb standing, as if slain, having seven horns and seven eyes, which are the seven Spirits of God, sent out into all the earth. And He came and took the book out of the right hand of Him who sat on the throne. When He had taken the book, the four living creatures and the twenty-four elders fell down before the Lamb, each one holding a harp and golden bowls full of incense, which are the prayers of the saints. And they sang a new song, saying,

    Worthy are You to take the book and to break its seals; for You were slain, and purchased for God with Your blood men from every tribe and tongue and people and nation. You have made them to be a kingdom and priests to our God; and they will reign upon the earth."

- **Revelation 11:15-16**

    Then the seventh angel sounded; and there were loud voices in heaven, saying, " The kingdom of the world has become the kingdom of our Lord and of His Christ; and He will reign forever and ever." And the twenty-four elders, who sit on their thrones before God, fell on their faces and worshiped God

- **Revelation 12:10**

  "Now the salvation, and the power, and the kingdom of our God and the authority of His Christ have come, for the accuser of our brethren has been thrown down, he who accuses them before our God day and night."

- **Revelation 12:17**

  So the dragon was enraged with the woman, and went off to make war with the rest of her children, who keep the commandments of God and hold to the testimony of Jesus.

In the next chapter, we will see why the enemy is so intent on wiping out the Covenant Community. His desire across history has been the genocide of the Jews because they would bear the Messiah into the world. But the Dragon and the Antichrist also want the genocide of the New Testament Covenant Community.

In the chapter to come we will see the very powerful and thrilling reason the Dragon wants the destruction of the Remnant Community, the Church of Jesus Christ.

Prior to Israel the nations saw time as completely cyclical—an endless, hopeless rotation of birth, death, rebirth-reincarnation forever. But through God's revelation entrusted to the Hebrew heart, history was revealed as also linear, meaning its circling events were not static, but moving forward toward goal and purpose—the coming of Messiah and the new heavens and the new earth foreseen by Hebrew prophets.

Chapter 6

THE REAL CHURCH IS A THREAT

The most insignificant nation in the world is the one no other power fears or wants to make war upon because it would be overkill, a waste of resources. That's why we never read sabre-rattling headlines about Luxembourg, Monaco, Nauru, Tuvalu, San Marino, Andorra, or Liechtenstein.

Some of them tag themselves as "grand", as in "The Grand Duchy of Luxembourg". But none of the great powers has such states as items in their defense budgets.

The same concept applies to sports teams. The coach of a top ten football team wouldn't spend much time readying his players to confront Piney Branch Mortuary College (if there be one) as he would another championship team.

There are some games that just don't count.

This is true on the cosmic scale. Every discipline of study and human institution sees there is something wrong with the world and is out to find what it is and what they can do about it.

Science can ultimately unravel the universe's riddles and solve humanity's problems, declare the contemporary Four Horsemen of Atheism—Richard Dawkins, Sam Harris, Daniel Dennett, and the late Christopher Hitchens.

Philosophers often believe they too can save the world. Karl Marx sought to convince humanity communism is the answer, Ayn Rand proposed radical rugged individualism as the solution, and Jean-Paul Sartre told us to jettison it all for the sake of the experience of the moment.

Education has been much ballyhooed as the savior. Horace Mann was certain public education would bring humanity out of darkness. John Dewey saw the utility of the child as the perpetuator of progress and produced disciples who would consider the ward of the state as much as the parent (and sometimes more).

Politicians and their governing regimes are always going to solve the challenges we face. Progressivists will give the governed policies that will stuff their pots with chickens, their garages with cars, and put a song on their lips.

Religions and their leaders meet in confabs with high-sounding names, issue richly worded resolutions and proclamations for the world's well-being, all the while thinking someone is listening.

Business and the marketplace promise to fabricate ever newer bells and whistles to drive away our misery and keep us in perpetual happiness.

The point of attack

But the powers of the Second Heaven do not make war on any of these—not science, or philosophy, or education, or government, or even religion. The dragon and the fallen angels know the only opponent that counts is the Covenant Community, the *ekklesia,* the called-out people of God living in the midst of the world as the truth threat to the regime of darkness.

The authentic church is the army of the Third Heaven operating in the First Heaven against the forces of the Second Heaven in their attempt to rule the First Heaven.

For the dragon and his minions, this is the only game in town, the only war worth fighting. So, says Revelation 12:17, once Satan realized he could not destroy Israel, he was in a state of enraging frustration, "and went off to make war with the rest of her children, who keep the commandments of God and hold to the testimony of Jesus."

Not the scientists, not the philosophers, not the educators, not the political powers, not the religious leaders— but the church, that body of "not many wise according to the flesh, not many mighty, not many noble"... the weak, the debased, the despised... those who "are not", who don't even exist in the eyes and minds of the world's great ones. (1 Corinthians 1:26-31)

The powers of the Second Heaven make war on the authentic church because it alone holds the "Keys of the Kingdom". (Matthew 16:19) The real church, the Covenant Community, is the sole entity in the First Heaven with the authority and strength of the Third Heaven to resist the attacks of the powers of the Second Heaven on the First Heaven.

I grasped this the first time as a 30-year old aide in the Nixon White House. I had been caught up in the secular frenzy of the 1960s, and abandoned my call to church ministry so I could do something "relevant" like working in the political sphere.

But as I watched the hopelessness in the White House, Congress, and Judiciary, I saw they were populated not only by "men without chests" (to borrow C.S. Lewis' great descriptor) but without heads as well. To my great shock and disappointment I realized government was not savior.

As I became more deeply involved with a White House prayer group I discovered what went on around that table of intercession was much more important than what was occurring in the Oval Office on the floor above. I left the White House in 1973 with the growing conviction that *the real church of Jesus Christ is the most potent organism in the world.*

Suddenly it hit me: The church is where the action is!

Must be stopped!

The dragon knows this. At all costs, he must stop the church. He recognizes it as Jesus-centered, Spirit-energized, Word-anchored, and Kingdom-envisioning. That means the Covenant Community is the agency for the advance of the Kingdom of God into all the world's arenas of engagement.

Cosmic government is in view in Revelation 12. Each of the "Heavens" are seats of authority—thrones and those who occupy them. However, God, enthroned in the Third Heaven, is the Supreme Ruler. All others are mere regents, holding power for a while either by God's direct intent or by His permission. Ultimately all the "Heavens" will be folded into the Third Heaven, and all will be reconciled to God, one in Him and His Kingdom.

Therefore, only God can grant authority to rule anywhere in whatever reality exists in the universe we inhabit and beyond. God has given that authority in the First Heaven only to His image-bearers, His regents in that 'territory' that encompasses all natural creation.

The Second Heaven is an imposition, with Lucifer *seizing* power from the Most High rather than its being *granted* to him. (But Lucifer can only "seize" power from God because God permits it.) This explains why Lucifer, the beautiful angel who becomes a beast—the dragon—is so intent on making war on the Covenant Community.

There is sequence to this war. Yet it is difficult to speak of "sequence" in this context because sequence has to do with the relativity of space and time, and the Holy Spirit through the Bible is revealing to us content from the perspective of the Absolute Realm.

Because we are finite beings we cannot comprehend fully the nature of the Absolute. Yet when we receive Jesus

Christ His Holy Spirit indwells the core of our being, the Holy of Holies called the human spirit. All humans have "eternity" in their hearts (Ecclesiastes 3:11) but in Christ our Holy Spirit-indwelt human spirit is seated in (Third) "heavenly places".

In our spirit we have the Mind of Christ, meaning we can now see into the Third Heaven in a limited way (limited because two-thirds of our being continues to be limited by the finite—our souls and bodies) This is the meaning of 1 Corinthians 13:9-12:

> For we know in part and we prophesy in part; but when the perfect comes, the partial will be done away. When I was a child, I used to speak like a child, think like a child, reason like a child; when I became a man, I did away with childish things. For now we see in a mirror dimly, but then face to face; now I know in part, but then I will know fully just as I also have been fully known.

But until the "perfect" (the *telos*, or purpose of all things) comes, we try to impose on our view of the Infinite-Absolute the limitations of the Finite-Relative perspective. That's why we see through a "glass" of warped, fogged-over mirror "dimly".

So, against that "epistemological" (how we know what we know) backdrop, let's review what the Bible shows us:

1. **Prior to the creation of the world and relative space and time (kronos), Lucifer launches an assault on the Throne of the Most High God in the realm of the absolute—the Third Heaven.**

Both Newtonian physics and Einstein's theory of relativity infer or speak of absolute space-time and relative space-time. Absolute space-time is reality at rest, not moving toward destruction, and infinite both in time and space.

We have spoken of absolute time as *kairos*. The Realm of Absolute Reality is therefore a continuum, a state of constancy of *being*, which is not dependent on kronos-time.

Relative space-time is reality in motion, a discontinuous, fitful convulsing of *function* from a point of beginning to a terminal point. It is totally dependent on tensed kronos-time. It is finite spatially and temporally (with reference to time, kronos).

The kronos-universe is relative in two senses. First, with respect to the relationship of objects in space and their effects on one another and the whole of the universe, as Einstein showed. The second relativity factor is that of kronos-time, which is affected by distance and velocity. The realm of relative space-time is therefore sequential (sequences leading to its finality).

Lucifer's rebellion starts in the Absolute Realm, the Third Heaven, plunges into the Second Heaven, where he establishes a base of operations from which he can launch assaults on the First Heaven. Ultimately, as we will see, Lucifer loses this strategic base and is cast down into earth itself.

2. Lucifer falls from the Third Heaven

Isaiah 14 and Ezekiel 28 speak of this as well as Luke 10:18 and Revelation 12. In that fall, Lucifer takes a third of the angels with him

3. Lucifer's fall requires the existence of a medium into which he can fall.

We have seen that a "heaven" (ouranos) is not only an expanse, but the seat of a throne. It is therefore a dominion, which is exactly what Colossians 1:13-14 shows us, as Paul writes that God "rescued us from the domain of darkness, and transferred us to the kingdom of His beloved Son , in whom we have redemption, the forgiveness of sins." The Second Heaven is a fragment, an off-shoot of the Absolute, permitted by the gracious Father Who grants freedom to all He creates

4. **God creates because He loves and wants all He creates to enter the loving fellowship of the Trinity, and therefore creates a realm populated by beings in His own Image, meaning they can enter into a relationship with the whole of God.**

That realm is the First Heaven. There is nothing Lucifer wants more than to displace God as the rightful King over that realm and impose his own rule there. Sadly, the first Adam, to whom the Most High God gave the right of rulership in the First Heaven, turned over that dominion to Lucifer. But because Adam's regency was limited in time, God will eventually re-enter the relative domain to reclaim it and refashion it into its original condition. Until then, through Christ the Son, God the Father raises up a people who will enter Covenant with Him, be filled with His Holy Spirit so they can enjoy the "firstfruits" of the coming Kingdom, and be His Kingdom "ambassadors" in the First Heaven.

And that brings us back to Revelation 12.

The Covenant Community is that remnant that continues to walk in the covenant of blood struck in history with Abraham, and fulfilled in the descendant of Abraham's line, Jesus of Nazareth, the Christ.

As we saw above, the first Adam turned over his dominion in the First Heaven to Lucifer when he appeared in the Garden and seduced Adam and Eve. Jesus, in John 12:31, recognizes Satan as the "ruler of this world", but stresses that this is a temporary rule because this usurper "will be cast out." As Jesus contemplates the cross He is about to endure, He says, "the ruler of this world is coming, and he has nothing in Me."

Always when Jesus speaks of Satan as the "ruler" of the present world the context is the limitation of satanic dominion in the created realm. Thus says Jesus in John 16:11, "the ruler of this world has (already) been judged." On the kairological plane the verdict has been laid down on Satan and the sentence of death declared, and all that waits is for the kairological reality of Satan's judgment and destruction to be manifest on the kronological level.

However, John will write, until Satan's defeat is fully manifest in kronos-time "the whole world lies in the power of the evil one." (1 John 5:18-19). The Dragon's temporary dominion is part of the "spillover effect" into the First Heaven of the conflict in the Second Heaven.

However, the Second Adam, Jesus Christ, brought the rule of the Kingdom with Him, and gave it to all who would be restored to the Covenant through His Blood. "If I by the finger of God cast out demons than the Kingdom of God has come among you," Jesus says to the Pharisees. However, the Kingdom has arrived in "seed" form, and its advance in the world will occur over the stretch of kronos-time that we call history.

During that span, it is the Covenant Community that holds dominion in the First Heaven. Therefore Revelation opens with the dedication:

To Him who loves us and released us from our sins by His blood — and He has made us to be a kingdom, priests to His God and Father — to Him be the glory and the dominion forever and ever. Amen. (Revelation 1:5-7 NASU)

Revelation 5:9-10 is even more direct. Christ has "purchased" with His blood people "from every tribe and tongue and people and nation" and "made them to be a kingdom and priests to our God; and *they will reign upon the earth*." (emphasis added) Ultimately, "the kingdom of the world" will "become the kingdom of our Lord and of His Christ" who "will reign forever and ever." (Revelation 11:15).

Until that happens the Covenant Community will represent the interests of God's Kingdom in the world. (Matthew 21:43; 2 Corinthians 5:20) Therefore, says Revelation 12:10, "the salvation, and the power, and *the kingdom of our God and the authority of His Christ have come*, for the accuser of our brethren has been thrown down, he who accuses them before our God day and night." (emphasis added)

This is why the Dragon, in raging frustration at his inability to destroy the "woman" goes off "to make war with the rest of her children, who keep the commandments of God and hold to the testimony of Jesus." (Revelation 12:17) The fusion of "commandments of God" and "the testimony of Jesus" show this to be completed Israel, the "cosmic Israel" that consists of the Old Covenant brought to its *pleroma,* or fullness in Christ and the New Covenant.

To understand the desperation of the Dragon to wipe out the (New) Covenant Community we must reach back into time, and Solomon's dedication of the Jerusalem Temple. 2 Chronicles 7:11-22 reveals:

> Thus Solomon finished the house of the LORD and the king's palace, and successfully completed all that he had planned on doing in the house of the LORD and in his palace. Then the LORD appeared to Solomon at night and said to him, "I have heard your prayer and have chosen this place for Myself as a house of sacrifice. If I shut up the heavens so that there is no rain, or if I command the locust to devour the land, or if I send pestilence among My people, and My people who are called by My name humble themselves and pray and seek My face and turn from their wicked ways, then I

will hear from heaven, will forgive their sin and will heal their land. Now My eyes will be open and My ears attentive to the prayer offered in this place. For now I have chosen and consecrated this house that My name may be there forever, and My eyes and My heart will be there perpetually. As for you, if you walk before Me as your father David walked, even to do according to all that I have commanded you, and will keep My statutes and My ordinances, then I will establish your royal throne as I covenanted with your father David, saying, ' You shall not lack a man to be ruler in Israel.' But if you turn away and forsake My statutes and My commandments which I have set before you, and go and serve other gods and worship them, then I will uproot you from My land which I have given you, and this house which I have consecrated for My name I will cast out of My sight and I will make it a proverb and a byword among all peoples. As for this house, which was exalted, everyone who passes by it will be astonished and say, ' Why has the LORD done thus to this land and to this house?' And they will say, 'Because they forsook the LORD, the God of their fathers who brought them from the land of Egypt, and they adopted other gods and worshiped them and served them; therefore He has brought all this adversity on them.'"

Sadly, Solomon and Israel do turn away from God, but the 'Temple' will be continued in and through the Covenant Community 'called out' from the world—the *ekklesia* (church). Therefore Jesus tells the leaders of Judaism,

"Did you never read in the Scriptures,

'The stone which the builders rejected,
this became the chief corner stone;
this came about from the Lord,
and it is marvelous in our eyes'?

"Therefore I say to you, the kingdom of God will be taken away from you and given to a people, producing the fruit of it. And he who falls on this stone will be broken to pieces; but on whomever it falls, it will scatter him like dust." (Matthew 21:42-44)

Thus there will come a day when "all Israel" (alive at that point in kronos-time) will be saved (Romans 11:26), but until it does, the genuine Church—the called-out remnant Covenant community—will have the authority to resist the dragon's attempts to maintain his power in the First Heaven.

THE ENEMY IS INTENSE BECAUSE HE KNOWS
HIS TIME IS RAPIDLY DRAWING TO A CLOSE,
THAT HIS WINDOW OF OPPORTUNITY IS
GETTING MORE AND MORE NARROW. SATAN
KNOWS SOMETHING BIG IS AHEAD—THE
COMING AGAIN OF THE TRUE MASTER OF
ALL CREATION, AND THE NEW HEAVENS AND
THE NEW EARTH!

Chapter 7

THE GREAT VICTORY

The greatest of enterprises, including a human life, most often comes down to a single sentence.

After the surrender of the Nazis and the end of the war in Europe Winston Churchill made a statement to Parliament, but it all came down to a sentence at the end, which he addressed to the leader of the House of Commons:

> I ... beg, Sir, with your permission to move:
>
> "That this House do now attend at the Church of St. Margaret, Westminster, to give humble and reverent thanks to Almighty God for our deliverance from the threat of German domination."

Churchill noted that was the exact motion that had been offered years earlier at the end of the First World War.

Less than a month earlier, on April 9, 1945, the great German pastor-theologian, Dietrich Bonhoeffer, was led to the gallows to be executed for his opposition to Hitler. In fact, the hanging was carried out at Hitler's explicit command. Bonhoeffer knew his killing by the Nazis was not his defeat, but his victory. Bonhoeffer's last words: *"This the end; for me the beginning of life."*

All the wars for justice and liberation fought in the entirety of the world's history could not come close to the strategic importance of the War in Heaven, and the great victory of Christ and His Kingdom.

The freedom, security, and hopes—not just of one small segment of history and humanity—but of the whole cosmos depended on the outcome of the war in heaven.

And it all came down to one sentence, spoken by Jesus at the end of His ordeal on the cross:

IT IS FINISHED!

Jesus' victory over the powers of the Second Heaven on the cross is the context for Revelation 12:7-12

> And there was war in heaven, Michael and his angels waging war with the dragon. The dragon and his angels waged war, and they were not strong enough, and there was no longer a place found for them in heaven. And the great dragon was thrown down, the serpent of old who is called the devil and Satan, who deceives the whole world; he was thrown down to the earth, and his angels were thrown down with him. Then I heard a loud voice in heaven, saying, "Now the salvation, and the power, and the

kingdom of our God and the authority of His Christ have come, for the accuser of our brethren has been thrown down, he who accuses them before our God day and night. And they overcame him because of the blood of the Lamb and because of the word of their testimony, and they did not love their life even when faced with death. For this reason, rejoice, O heavens and you who dwell in them. Woe to the earth and the sea, because the devil has come down to you, having great wrath, knowing that he has only a short time."

It is at the moment that Jesus cries out, "It is finished!" that "the salvation, and the power, and the kingdom of our God and the authority of His Christ have come..." into the world.

We see this in the meaning of Jesus's words, and several other passages that give us the "backstory"—a glimpse into what was behind those words.

Let's start with the report from John's Gospel:

After this, Jesus, knowing that all was now finished (ended), said in fulfillment of the Scripture, I thirst. [Ps 69:21.] A vessel (jar) full of sour wine (vinegar) was placed there, so they put a sponge soaked in the sour wine on [a stalk, reed of] hyssop, and held it to [His] mouth. When Jesus had received the sour wine, He said, It is finished! And He bowed His head and gave up His spirit. (John 19:28-30 AMP)

Jesus knew it all

The lead-in to the last word is the fact that Jesus knew "all was now finished." Until it was done He would not try to ease His thirst, and waits until His mission is completed before asking for a drink. Immediately after He had said that He shouts, "It is finished."

How do I know He shouted the words? Because of their meaning in Greek, *tetelestai.* The root is *telos,* or "purpose". The Latin translation is *consummatum est*, the matter is completed, consummated. This is not something Jesus would weakly say, but, if He still had the voice, would have shouted it.

Tetelestai would be written on a business document, and would be the equivalent of "paid in full".

Tetelestai is not a concession, but a proclamation. It is not the admission of defeat, but the declaration of victory. Satan has been cast down, and is no longer able to have a free go at humanity. He is cast down, and there is now the ability to resist him and even go after him. He is cast down, and now can be displaced, pushed aside.

Satan is cast down and now salvation is come into the earth, with all the power (*dunamis*) and authority (*exousia*) of the Kingdom of God. Now the people given this power and authority by Jesus Christ through the Holy Spirit can overcome the demonic powers of the Second Heaven by the Blood of the Lamb, the word of their testimony ("Christ is Lord" of my life and of all), and the fact they value Jesus Christ and His Kingdom even above their lives.

Why? Because Jesus did what He came into the world to do.

An anonymous writer reminds us:

> As Spurgeon says TETELESTAI conveys "an ocean of meaning in a drop of language, a mere drop. It would need all the other words that ever were spoken, or ever can be spoken, to explain this one word. It is altogether immeasurable. It is high; I cannot attain to it. It is deep; I cannot fathom it. IT IS FINISHED is the most charming note in all of Calvary's music. The fire has passed upon the Lamb. He has borne the whole of the wrath that was due to His people. This is the royal dish of the feast of love."
>
> J.C. Ryle wrote that "It is surely not too much to say, that of all the seven famous sayings of

Christ on the cross, none is more remarkable than TETELESTAI."

A.C. Gaebelein adds "Never before and never after was ever spoken ONE WORD which contains and means so much. It is the shout of the mighty Victor. And who can measure the depths of this ONE WORD!"

A.W. Pink writes that "Eternity will be needed to make manifest all that TETELESTAI contains." Matthew Henry described TETELESTAI as a "comprehensive word and a comfortable one."

Charles Simeon adds that 'since the foundation of the world there never was a single word uttered, in which such diversified and important matter was contained. Every word indeed that proceeded from our Saviour's lips deserves the most attentive consideration: but TETELESTAI eclipses all. To do justice to it, is beyond the ability of men or angels: its height, and depth, and length, and breadth, are absolutely unsearchable."[8]

The 'backstory'

Other passages give us the "backstory." Look at Ephesians 4:4-10:

> We are all one body, we have the same Spirit, and we have all been called to the same glorious future. There is only one Lord, one faith, one baptism, and there is only one God and Father, who is over us all and in us all and living through us all. However, he has given each one of us a special gift according to the generosity of Christ. That is why the Scriptures say,
> "When he ascended to the heights,
>   he led a crowd of captives
>   and gave gifts to his people."

Notice that it says "he ascended." This means that Christ first came down to the lowly world in which we live. The same

---

[8]   http://preceptaustin.wordpress.com/2013/04/05/tetelestai-it-is-finished-paid-in-full/

one who came down is the one who ascended higher than all the heavens, so that his rule might fill the entire universe. NLT

The Holy Spirit helps us understand why there was "war in heaven" in the first place—because the rule of the Victor, the Lord Jesus Christ, will fill the whole universe. This will displace, crush, and obliterate the Second Heaven and all its pretenses of power and hopes of universal domination.

Go to Rome today and you can still see the triumphal arches of Constantine, Severus, and Titus. Once they marched in victory after their battles, with all their foes now made captives, and trailing behind.

What captures us? The world, the flesh, the devil, and the lust of the flesh, the lust of the eyes and the pride of life. These enslave us, until we want to cry out with Paul, in Romans 7, "who shall deliver me from the body of this death?"

But now, because Satan has been cast down, captivity is itself captive, because salvation and the power and authority of God's Kingdom have come to the earth we can also with Paul, as he answered his own question, "Thanks be to God through Jesus Christ our Lord!" (Romans 7:25)

Another passage that provides "backstory" to *tetelestai* and Revelation 12 is Colossians 2:12-15—

When you came to Christ, you were "circumcised," but not by a physical procedure. It was a spiritual procedure — the cutting away of your sinful nature. For you were buried with Christ when you were baptized. And with him you were raised to a new life because you trusted the mighty power of God, who raised Christ from the dead. You were dead because of your sins and because your sinful nature was not yet cut away. Then God made you alive with Christ. He forgave all our sins. He canceled the record that contained the charges against us. He took it and destroyed it by nailing it to Christ's cross. In this way, God disarmed the evil rulers and authorities. He shamed them publicly by his victory over them on the cross of Christ. NLT

The Greek words translated "cancelled" with respect to our list of sins means to wipe it out completely so there's not even a trace left. That's *tetelestai,* a total completion or finish. Satan the accuser has been cast down because his very ground for attack has been taken from him.

"Disarm" is a Greek word meaning not only to strip an enemy of his weapons but also his clothes. Not only is the enemy made harmless, but disgraced as well.

Nagging postscript

Despite this immense cosmic victory there is a nagging little postscript to Revelation 12:

> And when the dragon saw that he was thrown down to the earth, he persecuted the woman who gave birth to the male child. But the two wings of the great eagle were given to the woman, so that she could fly into the wilderness to her place, where she was nourished for a time and times and half a time, from the presence of the serpent. And the serpent poured water like a river out of his mouth after the woman, so that he might cause her to be swept away with the flood. But the earth helped the woman, and the earth opened its mouth and drank up the river which the dragon poured out of his mouth. So the dragon was enraged with the woman, and went off to make war with the rest of her children, who keep the commandments of God and hold to the testimony of Jesus. (Revelation 12:13-17)

In previous chapters we talked about how the numerous attempts across history to eradicate the Jews have failed. In the last chapter we explored why Satan is so determined to destroy the "offspring" of the woman who follow Jesus—the genuine church. It is because of all the entities and agencies in the world only the authentic church has the power and authority of the Kingdom.

When Satan was cast down, salvation and the power and authority of the Kingdom came down too. And the keys of the power and authority of the Kingdom were given to the true church.

So if the enemy is defeated why is the battle here on earth still raging? The answer is in Revelation 12:12, "Woe to the earth and the sea, because the devil has come down to you, having great wrath, knowing that he has only a short time."

This is among the reasons I am so fascinated by the Normandy Invasions. The moment the Allies landed, the war was over for Hitler and the Nazis. Hitler's top generals knew it, and began trying to figure out how to save their hides. But Hitler refused to believe it, and so the war raged on.

The victory was established first in the villages and cities along the Normandy coast, and then into France and the Low Countries, and ultimately into Germany itself. But the victory had to be taken village to village, town by town, region by region until the whole nation experienced liberation.

The Nazis threw up desperate and heavy opposition at the Battle of the Bulge—their last great hope of stopping the

Allied onslaught. So today we in the church are not fighting to achieve victory, but to take the victory to the ends of the earth.

The cosmic "Normandy Invasion" was the first coming of Jesus and His Kingdom. What we are fighting now is like the battles to take the victory to Caen and Rouen, Paris and Lyon, to Frankfurt and Heidelberg, and ultimately to Berlin, the center of the enemy's control.

These struggles are costly and bloody. There have been more martyrs for Christ in our lifetimes than in all of previous history. Right now there is vicious persecution of the church at unprecedented levels. Those of us not shedding literal blood are having our character and reputation, opportunities and freedoms assaulted. The Western culture that benefitted so much from the Gospel of the Kingdom is now rejecting it, and even hating it and those who embrace it, follow it, and proclaim it.

The enemy is intense because he knows his time is rapidly drawing to a close, that his window of opportunity is getting more and more narrow.

Satan knows something big is ahead—the Coming again of the true Master of all creation, and the new heavens and the new earth!

www.ingramcontent.com/pod-product-compliance
Lightning Source LLC
Chambersburg PA
CBHW021828090426
42811CB00032B/2068/J